SPEEDWAY
AT FULL THROTTLE

SPEEDWAY
AT FULL THROTTLE

CHAPLIN AND SOMERVILLE

HALSGROVE

First published in Great Britain in 2017
Copyright © John Chaplin and John Somerville 2017

A CIP record for this title is available from the British Library

ISBN 978 0 85704 307 8

HALSGROVE
Halsgrove House,
Ryelands Business Park,
Bagley Road, Wellington, Somerset TA21 9PZ
Tel: 01823 653777   Fax: 01823 216796
email: sales@halsgrove.com

Part of the Halsgrove group of companies.
Information on all Halsgrove titles is available at: www.halsgrove.com

Printed and bound by Parksons Graphics, India

CONTENTS

For

DAVE LANNING

1938 - 2016

The voice of Speedway

*The Dave Lanning style. Always where the action is,
interviewing Peter Collins immediately after he had become
World Champion at Chrozow in 1976.*

AUTHORS' NOTE

THE full possibilities of speedway racing have yet to be sounded, for the sport lives and has its being in the enthusiasm of the people. *TOM STENNER from Thrilling The Million: The Lure Of The Speedway 1934*

CELEBRATING A JUBILEE

FIRST, a confession. This book is based on the *Museum Piece* series John Somerville and I have contributed to *Speedway Star* magazine for some years. But it wasn't my original idea. I stole it from the man who set me on the road to speedway journalism, my literary idol and mentor Basil Storey.

Maybe I should say I resurrected it rather than stole it because *Museum Piece* first appeared in Basil's *Speedway Gazette* in 1949. I was then a youthful fan of 15 who had discovered speedway three years earlier. Now, 68 years later, I am still as captivated by it's history, and the men and women who forged it into the global sport it is today, as I was then.

At the time I was eager to know how it all came about because the sport of dirt-track racing was then a mere 21 years old and many of the magnificent originals were still around to tell their tales, some were actually riding and continuing to thrill the million.

Dear old Basil laid it all out for me, and others like me, with his unique style of writing that somehow encapsulated the romance, drama, heroism, glamour and bravery of the sport, its practitioners and culture. His words on the printed page brought to life the colour, that distinctive methanol/Castrol-R smell and every spectacular, thrilling magnificent moment that is speedway racing. Equally as important was the way he would weave his magic to create the star personalities who he turned into the sporting celebrities of the time.

Basil and the old *Speedway Gazette* are now long gone, but thanks to his inspirational skill, eventually – with much perseverance, patience and dedication to breaking through into speedway journalism – I found myself writing a gossip column (talking point was forbidden) for the forerunner of *Speedway Star* (the pay was fifteen shillings, amounting to 75pence, for a thousand words). But, more than money, it meant I was actually allowed into the racing pits during a meeting where, probably open mouthed and certainly in awe, I was privileged to be in the actual presence of the living, breathing, leather clad heroes of the track.

So Basil has a lot to answer for, and many are the cinders and much shale has been shifted since those days. My speedway journalistic career has been considerable, exactly 60 years, it has been eventful, rewarding, satisfying, uplifting and sometimes, inevitably because it is the nature of the sport, grief- stricken and sad. This book is for me, and I hope you, a fitting Diamond Jubilee with which to celebrate that very long and continually winding road.

Without doubt the most rewarding and satisfying times have been during my comparatively recent association with the Master Photographic Guru John Somerville. He has, rightly, an unenviable worldwide reputation for the way he has amassed his unique archive of historic speedway pictures, and indeed continues to do so.

John is a reporter's dream. He is utterly wonderful to work with. He is totally unselfish, has a much tidier mind than me and a fantastic filing system. It has been my very great and infinite pleasure to have been associated with him over the past few years.

From the Poor Wee Sassenach, to the Poor Wee Scot (*we both know it sure aint made us rich*), thanks a milliion John. There are no other words for it . . . you are The Best.

John Chaplin
Stamford, Lincolnshire 2016

FOREWORD

PRECIOUS MEMORIES

MEMORY is a precious thing, as we grow older its value is incalculable and yet no matter how much we nurture it in order to preserve these treasurable recollections, they can dissolve into the mists of the time, sometimes never to be recalled again. Yet quite often it's when we blow the dust off of a long forgotten photo album, or an old shoe box that's been retrieved from the dark recesses of a cupboard that the memories suddenly come flooding back – and the stories.

And this latest book from John Chaplin and John Somerville aims to do just that. Somerville the wide-eyed collector of visual delights is your prompter, and Chaplin the teller of brave tales of men and machines, of triumph and tragedy, of success and failure.

I have come to know both of these men quite well in my own scribbling career. They continue to preserve the memories and deeds of this sport, ensuring that there is a record both written and visual of days gone by.

In more than 25-years of writing I have had many different editors, some only for a short time, others for longer. They've all been different; yet less than a handful have made a lasting impression, Indeed it was Chaplin who really gave me a start in speedway racing and it was he who also advised, encouraged and corrected me as the editor/publisher of the *Vintage Speedway Magazine*.

Chaplin is what I call a proper journalist, a veteran of Fleet Street, he was like no other editor I had known at that time and what he didn't know was that I was a bit of a fan. I used to look for his by-line in the various speedway publications of the period, just as I did others like Mick Wall in rock music and Michael Scott in motorcycle racing, because he was often writing about the men that I was interested in and he'd reveal information that others seldom got close to discovering.

So his suggestions, sometimes painful to digest, were taken on board and put into practice until one day I was rewarded with a lead feature where he hadn't altered a word. I can still remember my sense of achievement because he never taught me in a classroom-like environment, it was all done from the editor's chair, so it was very much down to me, and me alone, to take notice of what he was doing, and why, to create tighter and better copy. I was a little man with big ideas and with John's guidance I was able to realise some of them.

Later I worked for others who were sticklers in a way that the modern wordsmiths cannot possibly begin to appreciate judging by the standards that are now considered to be the norm. John wouldn't allow that sort of cliché-ridden sloppiness, which has obviously arrived with the laziness of the internet generation, and even now he'll offer his experience – although it is done from a different seat of observation.

John Somerville is an enthusiast, an Edinburgh Monarchs supporter, a collector and an unsung hero of speedway racing. It was while I was working on some historical articles I first came into contact with him. At that time his collection, for which he had acquired the copyright, was mainly photos from Wright Wood. Since then it has grown considerably to around one million images, spanning the sport's history in the UK and abroad featuring top photographers including the award-winning Mike Patrick and Alf Weedon.

Today 'The John Somerville Collection' is the place to go for all editors and publishers who are covering speedway. The fact that these images are gathered altogether in one place is a massive boost for all fans.

The significance of capturing a vivid moment was recently underlined when film-maker Steven Spielberg indicated that the inspiration behind his Oscar-winning movie, Saving Private Ryan (1998), came from the now famous picture by Robert Cappa of a GI moving through the sea toward the Normandy beaches during the D-Day landings in 1944. Part of a collection of images known as 'The Magnificent Eleven,' it's amazing that Cappa managed to take anything given the hostile environment he was in, never mind while trying to stay alive!

By comparison, the speedway photographer doesn't operate in such a dangerous setting as Cappa, but it's not without its risks or challenges. Remember until the late 1980s flash photography was not permitted in British speedway, a major drawback when you consider most of the meetings took place in the twilight hours when light was fading at best, never mind the dusty, dirty nature of the sport and, of course the speed. Moreover, no-one really worried about health and safety until recent years, yet there are few tales of snappers getting injured from the carnage that often occurs on track. Nevertheless, the fact that there are photos from every era is one thing, but to discover them to be in such impressive quality in conditions that would even challenge today's technically-advantaged photographers, says a lot about the talent of the men operating what were quite cumbersome machines.

Therefore, the partnership of Chaplin and Somerville, which has been established in previous books and the regular *Museum Piece* in *Speedway Star*, is the perfect combination to take you back through the sport's history and recall the famous, notorious and not-so famous characters, while reliving some of the glory days.

Brian Burford
Marlborough, Wiltshire

THE first thing I do when I get my copy of *Speedway Star* is look for Museum Piece. I really enjoy them, and so I was excited to learn about the new book by two of our very best speedway historians, John Chaplin and John Somerville. Having read other books with John Chaplin's words and John Somerville's great pictures, this latest based on their *Museum Pieces* is sure to be one speedway fans old and young will want to read.
OVE FUNDIN, Five times World Speedway Champion

JOHN CHAPLIN has spent a lifetime, spanning several decades, in journalism and throughout that period has devoted much of his time accumulating a huge knowledge of speedway's past, right back to its birth, and as such could rightly be called the sport's historian.
JOHN SOMERVILLE has proved to be the guardian angel of speedway's pictorial history, acquiring the vast photo collections of many of the great photographers including Wright Wood, Alf Weedon and Mike Patrick.
Chaplin's words and Somerville's photos make a potent cocktail for anyone with the slightest interest in speedway through the ages and especially a period when it was as popular as soccer and regularly attracted crowds in excess of 80,000 to Wembley Stadium for mere league meetings. Their *Museum Piece* series in *Speedway Star* has proved very popular and their latest collaboration will doubtless be so too given the quality of the material both bring to the table.
PHILIP RISING, MANAGING EDITOR, Speedway Star

INTRODUCTION

DIPPING ME LID...

WHEN you match the endeavours of two men who are unsurpassed in their fields, the result is an unsurpassed product.

That, my friends, is what you have with this book.

John Chaplin is renowned across the globe as speedway's unsurpassed historian. Even though I live 12,000 miles away in Sydney, whenever I (or my readers) want to know anything about speedway back in the days before the bubble burst and the sport was second only in spectator appeal to soccer, the go-to man is John Chaplin.

You can tell by his cute and youthful looks that he's been around for a loooong time. You don't gather so much experience, combined with so much expertise, without becoming an expert. And there is no greater expert in the field of speedway history than JC.

I once asked him what brand of cough mixture Aub Lawson was sipping in the West Ham pits circa 1947 between races when the Aussie great was suffering a cold. A picture was printed in the speedway press at the time. To this day I cannot believe JC actually knew the answer!. Is there nothing this man hasn't got covered? (It was, of course, Nyal).

So now that we've established John Chaplin's credentials as the man who knows almost as much about the past stars of speedway as even their better halves, and matched that wealth of knowledge with his accreditation as a Fleet Street journalist, you have the world's ultimate historical speedway author.

Chaplin puts his words together in that readable way so as you turn the pages you can almost smell the methanol and burning Castrol-R racing oil. I suggest that is sufficient, alone, to buy, savour and salivate over this book.

But the goodness doesn't end there.

Bring in John Somerville from Scotland and you've got a literary marriage made in heaven. Jock has put together the most stupendous collection of speedway photographs imaginable.

There have been no finer photographers in speedway than the incredibly talented Alf Weedon, Mike Patrick and Trevor Meeks. Before them came, of course, many other outstanding lensmen such as Wright Wood and C.F. Wallace.

Whoever would have thought, 10-20 years ago, that all their works would come together under the one umbrella? I would have seen it, literally, as a financial and logistic impossibility.

Jock has stunned the world of speedway by pulling off this totally amazing feat. I dread to think of the cost, but he's actually done it – he's bought and brought all those photo collections together to create an unsurpassed photographic arsenal of speedway's history from the 1920s to a tad before contemporary times.

If it was snapped between 1923 and 2000, you can bet John Somerville has it. He's even got my own speedway motorcycle and car collection from my five years as a professional speedway photographer around the tracks of Australia.

Again, like Chaplin, Somerville is the go-to man for anyone wanting photos from speedway's past. When I wrote my two books on the legends of Aussie speedway, where did I turn for shots of Vic Huxley, Vic Duggan, Jim Airey, Charlie Monk, (you get the drift)?

John Somerville of course. There is none other.

So if you put the best words together with the best photos, you get the best book. This, simply, is another must-have from the Chaplin-Somerville alliance. Buy it, read it and I'm sure you'll agree.

I dips me lid to both amazing gentlemen keeping the wonderful heritage alive book after book.

They've done it again!

Peter White
Australian speedway journalist for 54 years
Speedway Star *correspondent for 48 years*
Editor and publisher of **Speedway World** *(Australia) for 30 years*
(an Australian speedway publishing record)

THE ORIGINALS

SO HERE we go then, with *Speedway Gazette* Editor Basil Storey's original and my original . . . neither picture is of the highest quality, but their value is in their antiquity.

The very first *Museum Piece* appeared in *Speedway Gazette* dated 8 Ocober 1949. These are the 130 pearls of Storey wisdom:

THIS picture makes speedway racing history. The starting gate as we now know it was invented by New Cross promoter Fred Mockford and built for him by pre-war rider Harry Shepherd. Here you see the boys gathered around the gate at the New Cross track in 1934.

GAZETTE, OCTOBER 8, 1949—5

When Ron Johnson was just a hopeful boy: MUSEUM PIECE No. 1

This picture makes speedway racing history. The starting gate as we now know it was invented by New Cross promoter Fred Mockford and built for him by pre-war rider star Harry Shepherd. Here you see the boys gathered round the gate at the New Cross track in 1934.

Anyone recognise the two riders waiting for the tapes to fly up? On his machine extreme left is the late Tom Farndon and next to him is young Ron Johnson, present-day skipper of the Rangers. Standing behind Farndon is another old-time rider, Nobby Key. Others in the group include Harry Shepherd (fifth from left), Fred Mockford (half-hidden by post), and on the extreme right Tom Morgan.

This is the first picture in our grand new series entitled "Museum Piece."

Anyone recognise the two riders waiting for the tapes to fly up? On his machine extreme left is the late Tom Farndon and next to him is young Ron Johnson, present day skipper of the Rangers. Standing behind Farndon is another old time rider, Nobby Key. Others in the group include Harry Shepherd (fifth from left, Fred Mockford (half hidden by post), and on the extreme right journalist Tom Morgan.

This is the first picture in our grand news series entitled Museum Piece.

AND here are mine . . . 201 of them which appeared under the headline CHEETAH JOHNNIE and is dated January 2003.

SINCE this is the first of a series, let's start with a bit of fun! Perpetrated by that one and only Maestro Of Fun, the late and very great Johnnie Hoskins. In case you didn't know Johnnie claimed to be the father of speedway in Australia in 1923 – a claim that has so far resisted every attempt to discredit him.

He was also speedway's master showman, and during his fiery reign at West Ham before the war his interval attractions were legendary.

He packed the Custom House terraces with such diversions as camel and elephant races, but his attempt to match his riders against cheetahs, the fastest animals on earth, backfired.

During morning trials, Johnnie recalled: 'The brutes got loose, and my directors, fearing lawsuits and injuries to the public, made me cancel. But it was too late to advertise a non-appearance.'

Before a tremendous crowd the 'races' started – and ended after 30 yards when the cheetahs were halted by leather tethers. And Johnnie had to publicly confess he'd been the event's biggest 'cheetah'.

Hammers' post-war skipper Eric Chitty is pictured with one of the real ones.

There is more on the Old Windbag, Madcap Johnnie (Liar.Hons), later . . .

Chapter 1
HUNTING'S TEAM OF MADCAP MARAUDERS

THERE couldn't be a more distinguished line-up than this. They are the daring adventurers who first brought the sport half way across the world and really established speedway in Britain.

While not forgetting the brave English pioneers who put on such a spectacular show on that memorable day behind the King's Oak Hotel in Epping Forest in February 1928, when these boys with the kangaroos emblazened on their sweaters turned up they realised there was quite a lot to learn.

This picture was taken three years on from the High Beech bonanza. It's a strength-in-depth Australia ready to take on the Old Enemy. And every one of them is not only a maverick in the true Aussie tradition, but nowadays they would all be described as speedway superstars.

From the left they are Max Grosskreutz, Lionel Van Praag, Charlie Spinks, Len Woods, Frank Arthur, Ron Johnson and Billy 'Cyclone' Lamont.

Their leader out front was the biggest star of them all – Victor Nelson Huxley. Hux, in his way, was a sportsman with as formidable a reputation as any modern day motor sport champion. As a master of his art he was someone the crowds loved or hated in equal measure. He was ruthlessly successful and he pulled in the paying customers.

1931

Near the Toowoomba rail yards in 1927. A lot of the riders here were in AJ-Hunting's party of the original sixteen that went to England in 1928. From the left... AJ Hunting, (standing) .. Vic Huxley, on the front guard ...Lionel Van Praag, on the roof Hilary Buchanan in the cab... Guy Walker outside .. Fred Barber .. Colin Arnott ..Jock Binney ... Ben Unwin, and Stan Cooper

He came over in the first wave of A.J. Hunting's madcap marauders in early 1928. After weeks getting race rusty on board the boat from Australia, he disembarked in Italy and took the train to Paris. There he caught an Imperial Airways flight to Croydon and landed in England ready and eager for action.

A scant 24 hours later he was at the High Beech track having worked on a bike which had been supplied to him – complete with brakes, silencers and lights. Dirt track racing was very new to Britain and the locals knew little about the art of broadsiding – until Hux went into the cinder-smoking first bend at King's Oak and pomptly shattered the one and four lap track records.

The amazed crowd was stunned into silence at the spectacle. Until the times were announced, and then the fans went wild. Hux took it all in his stride. He was never known to lose his cool.

Modern enthusiasts may marvel at today's Grand Prix stars' stables of machinery, but even in those early days Hux kept up to seven bikes and two full time mechanics because he was in such demand that he was riding five and a half days – and sometimes nights as well – every week. It was not unknown for the big names to take part in two meetings a day.

It was, of course, only a matter of time before aspiring British riders began to match the skill and abilities of the Australian invaders. The breakthrough came in the year before this picture was taken, in 1930 when the first official Test series between England and Australia took place.

After an initial painful defeat at Wimbledon in the opening Test, England went on to win the next four that year. When they got around to the one pictured, the fourth match of the 1931 series at Belle Vue, the home side was leading by two matches to one.

They won this one too, even though in desperation the Aussies had recalled the legendary Lamont. The match report records that the Australians didn't cope with the track as well as the English riders. Conditions were 'rather treacherous' because of rain.

Final score: England 53 Australia 41. True to form, Huxley topped his side's score with ten points. England went on to post a 4 – 1 series win.

And this is the happy star spangled gathering at the outback outpost Toowoomba, most of Australia's original invasion force before setting out to conquer the world … first stop England.

The man who led his Madcap Marauders to the other side of the globe, A.J. Hunting, can be seen standing on the left holding on to the mudguard of that magnificent vehicle on which sits Vic Huxley. Lionel Van Praag is on the roof and among the others is Hilary Buchanan, in the cab, and Ben Unwin.

Chapter 2
HIMS ANCIENT AND MODERN

YOU could, in speedway terms, entitle this rather happy looking episode: *Hims Ancient And Modern.*

The Him on the left is America's first World Champion Jack Milne. *The Him* on the right is America's second World Champion, Bruce Penhall. And the US of A had spent 44 years in the speedway wilderness between the two triumphs.

Picture: Scott Dalosio USA.

What was happening was that veteran Jack was presenting Bruce with a special plaque, commemorating exactly what is not known. But Americans are very fond of bestowing such items on their sporting heroes. Whatever . . . both appear to be extremely delighted.

Bruce brought much-needed high profile glamour to the sport the world over and achieved idolatry status with his iconic win in the 1981 Wembley World Final. His delighted fans are seen to be embracing him ecstatically after his Wembley win as he took the championship trophy to show them.

But it all ended – quite abruptly – when he won again in Los Angeles the following year, then quit on the winner's rostrum for a (short-lived) acting career.

The more modest and unassuming Jack contributed in no less a way to speedway by aiding and abetting Harry Oxley to reignite the sport in the now famous little West Coast citadel Costa Mesa with the incorporated assistance of the Ivan Mauger-Barry Briggs know-how.

Jack more or less contented himself thereafter by assuming a behind-the-scenes role which included being Oxley's trackman. He once said: 'I leave all the shouting to Harry.

He likes to get out there in front of the people, he's just like Johnnie Hoskins.'

The Milne magic had first manifested itself in the mid-Thirties. The success of Jack and brother Cordy in America and Australia had been noted by New Cross mastermind Fred Mockford who brought the pair of them to England in 1936 as replacement for the brilliant Tom Farndon, killed the previous year. Farndon was not only New Cross's No.1, but acknowledged to be the uncrowned World No. 1 at the time.

An unseemly squabble then broke out among the top English promoters. The Speedway Control Board decided that New Cross would be too strong if both Jack and Cordy were allowed to ride for the same team, so Cordy was directed to the new Hackney Wick side.

Within weeks Jack had a crash at West Ham in a World Championship qualifier in which the thumb of his left hand was sliced off. A Custom House trackraker had promoter Hoskins near to swooning away by retrieving Jack's thumb from the cinders and presenting it to him in a matchbox.

At the time Jack was concerned that the loss of the digit would impair his performances. It didn't. He qualified for that First World Final in 1936, finishing ninth. The next year he was World Champion and he is seen taking the famous Wembley triumphant tractor ride with fellow American Wilbur Lamoreaux just behind him. Brother Cordy was third for an American clean sweep.

Soon afterwards Fred Mockford went along to ACU headquarters in Pall Mall to collect the World Championship trophy where it was being engraved with the winners' names. The inscriptions read: *'L. Van Praag, Wembley, 1936'*. And: *'J. Milne, Wembley, 1937'*.

Fred was outraged that the ACU panjandrums did not know which track Jack Milne rode for. Thoroughly disgusted, Fred refused to accept the trophy until the inscription was corrected. He stalked off with only the small replica trophy, which he later discovered had also been wrongly engraved.

So . . . whatever was inscribed on the plaque that Jack handed over to Bruce . . . we can only hope it was correct.

Chapter 3
THE MOORE MAGIC

HOW HE SURVIVED THE WALL OF DEATH AND A DEATH THREAT FROM THE 'CLAN'

MANY people have asked me over the years why I haven't written anything about Ronnie Moore. Well, of course I have, in Speedway Star and a book called **John Chaplin's Speedway Special** *in 1990.*

It was all thanks to a lovely lady named Dorothy Charles-Batson, probably Wimbledon's number one fan. She was 'Mum' to many aspiring riders and she adored Ronnie. Her double-barrelled name may have done no harm at all to his being awarded an MBE. She also dedicated a room in her home to the memory of the late Tommy Jansson.

At the time I was just starting to make my way, and Mrs Batson always encouraged me. At the same time she was never slow to express her feelings if she didn't approve of something I had written. But she must have approved of me the day she arranged for me to have a secret one-on-one interview with Ronnie. It was memorable and I am forever grateful. It really was a privilege.

RONNIE MOORE enjoyed a unique place in the hearts of the speedway going public far and away beyond the horizons of his New Zealand home in what he calls sleepy Christchurch.

If he ever thought that it might not be so it was proved beyond doubt when, having been away from British racing for seven years Mrs Batson wrote to the double World Champion on the other side of the globe and said she wanted to try and raise enough money to fly him to a grand reunion with his speedway pals.

Ronnie, fit again and rebuilding a future following the accident at Jerilderie Park which almost killed him, said it couldn't be done. He told Mrs Charles-Batson, in his usually

The Boy Wonder. A 17-year-old Ronnie and his father Les are welcomed to Wimbledon by captain and mentor Norman Parker.

natural modest way, that not enough people would remember him and, anyway, he had not even bothered to renew his passport.

Mrs B set to work at her Wimbledon home and, by the time she had finished, enough people had remembered Ronnie to stump up the price of a return air ticket with some left over for spending money. Not only that, there was also a car for his use and an Engllsh speedway travel company laid on a trip for him to see the World Final which was in Sweden that year.

Among the most generous donations were contributions from the two men whose practical concern had ensured he was able to cling to life when so gravely injured, fellow New Zealanders Barry Briggs and Ivan Mauger.

The universal and positive demonstration of affection when he arrived moved Ronnie to tears more than once during the trip. A few days later, when he had overcome his jet lag, he agreed to meet me.

***

THE first thing you do when you come face to face with Ronnie Moore is look for the damage. There is none to see. The only item about him that seems in any way untoward is the wholly unnaturally pink coloured miniature box located near an ear. It indicates that Ronnie needs mechanical

assistance to hear what you are saying to him.

'The damage is all inside,' he said, tapping the vicinity of his ear with a finger. 'All the nerves in there are shattered, and your balance depends on your hearing. But I've never had good hearing. It goes back to the days when I was a kid on the Wall Of Death. The noise factor.

'I'll never, ever, be properly all right again. I will have to take certain pills for the rest of my life, and I get dizzy spells. But that's no hardship, really, it means I can't go clambering about on roofs. I tried it and fell off. And of course, I daren't get on a speedway bike again . . . '

It happened on Monday, 20 January 1975. Ronnie was racing in the Australian round of the Mauger-Briggs World Champions Troupe series at Jerilderie Park, near Newcastle,

Moving on up. The youthful Ronnie starting to find his way in the tough English speedway world and learning fast.

New South Wales. At the age of 42 he was feeling well pleased with himself. He was beating the world's best still. Apart from the two principals, the Troupe included Anders Michanek and Tommy Jansson of Sweden, England's John Louis, Germany's Egon Muller, America's Scott Autrey and Ole Olsen of Denmark.

In his third ride of the night his front wheel hit a rut in the track which sent it skittering across the surface until it collided with the rear of John Louis's bike. Ronnie's handlebars were wrenched from his grip and struck him on the side of the head. This may not have been so catastrophic had he been wearing his full-face helmet. But a sneak thief had stolen if from a display in his motorcycle showroom just before he set out for Australia.

Ronnie was able to piece together what happened when he was struck by the bars. He said: 'The result was instant oblivion. The whole of the right side of my head was smashed in.'

Ivan Mauger was leading that fateful race and, when he arrived back at the scene of the accident, he was appalled to find track staff still attempting to remove Ronnie's helmet without first undoing the strap. Ivan brushed them aside and undid it himself.

Ronnie said: 'Ivan saved my life. He . . . pushed the track staff out of the way. He took off my helmet, pulled out my tongue, which I had swallowed and was choking on and

held my head in his lap until the ambulance arrived.

'After the meeting he and Barry rushed to the hospital to be informed I was as good as dead, and there was nothing they could do.

'Ivan arranged an ambulance and two police escorts and a mad dash to North Shore Hospital in Sydney, where they put a drill through my head, and that started getting things beating again.

'Naturally I knew nothing about this as I was in a coma for a long while.

'A couple of months later I was flown home to Christchurch and into the hospital there. After two weeks I discharged myself because I'd had enough of hospitals. My left ear was shattered and my right ear took two operations to get a little hearing back, but that was my balanced stuffed.

'A year later Ivan flew me to Newcastle for the same meeting so I could walk into the centre green and let the people see me moving. By asking a lot of people I found out all that Ivan had done to keep me in this world.

'I was flown over to Aussie for the speedway veterans' dinner in Sydney after Ivan said I had better get up to his place in Surfers Paradise because the Indy cars were going to race through the streets.

'A couple of days later he drove me up to Brisbane to catch a plane home, I got out of his car and said thanks, but he got out and gave me one hell of a hug that brought tears to my eyes. Since the crash I have seen the other side of Ivan that most people don't realise is there.'

After the accident Ronnie was unconscious for almost a month. Eventually he became well enough to ask his doctor how he was. The doctor snapped his fingers and told him: 'You were that close to dying.' Ronnie said: 'I can't describe the shock it gave me. I was afraid to move a muscle.'

When all the convalescing was done, Ronnie went back to his motorcycle business. They had told him first that it would take two years in hospital before be would be right. But he persuaded them to let him go home to see the FA Cup final on television – and he stayed the night. Then he went back to hospital to argue that if he could do it for one night, he could stay every night and attend hospital for treatment by day. They let him have his way.

He said: 'I was incapable of doing anything except sit and read and watch television . . . and think. I had a hell of a long time to think and to analyse things.'

He could think about and analyse a quarter of a century of involvement with speedway racing and it would have taken him through a veritable seven ages of man as he made his way from obscurity, as a small country circus performer in New Zealand to world fame as the most naturally gifted single individual to perform in the speedway arena.

At first he was the Boy Wonder who, at only 17, took the British speedway scene by storm and rode straight to the 1950 World Final at Wembley. His achievement ushered in a new wave of sparkling young talent, the natural inheritors of stardom from the fading pre-war dirt-track pioneers.

Then Ronnie became, next to Peter Craven, the sport's youngest World Champion at 21. His maturity launched Wimbledon into its Golden Age. Honours flooded in – seven National Trophies, seven League titles, World Champion again . . . then a brief flirtation with car racing.

'I enjoyed racing cars,' said Ronnie. 'With cars you had so many different circuits. With speedway you are on the track and turning left all the time. I did a year and then I started to win things. Aston Martin and Lotus wanted me to have a trial drive.

'At the time my wife was pregnant. She was in hospital and she was really bad. She

The homecoming. After seven years away he was given a rapturous welcome back by his old team mates and Dons supporters. Carrying him shoulder high are Barry Briggs (far left), Cyril Brine and on the right promoter Ronnie Greene and Cyril Maidment.

Decision time. Ronnie is forced to make a choice between representing Australia or New Zealand. He chooses New Zealand and joins up with, from left standing, Maury Dunn, Geoff Mardon, Ron Johnston, Barry Beriggs. Kneeling: Merv Neil, Trevor Redmond, Ronnie and Peter Clark.

Above: *Mature World Champions' gathering. Ronnie on the bike – naturally – Barry Briggs (centre) and Ivan Mauger with twelve titles between them.*

Right: *Going at it: Peter Craven on the outside with Ronnie hoping he has a mighty enough motor to keep up.*

asked me would I quit car racing. And I said: "Why?" She said: "In the first six meetings six of your friends got killed. In speedway, if you break a leg, and I hate that, but at least you're up and about. In cars if you have a bang, nine times out of ten you're dead." So basically I quit cars and went back to speedway.'

Eventually there was another injury and drop out – for six years. There had to be a 'for old time's sake' comeback and, at the veteran's age of 36, it was as if he had never been away. Thumbing his nose at the years, he took another world title, the Pairs with Ivan Mauger. Finally it was really all over.

There is a remarkable interview with Ronnie on You Tube, conducted by his fellow multi-World Champion Barry Briggs, during which Ronnie, so often monosyllabic when under close media questioning, opens up to tell how it really was for him.

It is fascinating to listen to Ronnie's comments and opinions on members of speedway's 'closed shop union' with which the original track stars jealously and forcefully protected their privileged position at the top. They were none too pleased that a sensational young interloper suddenly appeared among them to muscle in on their domain and openly challenge them. Especially one who was so obviously supremely talented.

During the interview Ronnie is persuaded to offer his forthright views on his

The brief flirtation with cars: 'I enjoyed racing cars . . . my wife said: "In cars, if you have a bang, nine times out of ten you're dead." So I quit'.

contemporaries and even some of the greats who emerged later.

The very young Ronnie had learned how to ride a motorcycle performing in his father Les's Wall Of Death show. Speedway all began for him in 1948 when he was 14. His father was riding on a local horse training track and one day he asked Ronnie if he would like to have a ride. Permission was cleared with the ACU and, Ronnie said: 'I went out and had a ride and it was exciting. When speedway started in Christchurch it was sort of automatic. Maybe I was just lucky, it seemed to click, fairly naturally.

'Then, a couple of years later Norman Parker came out and started telling me a few little things.' Wimbledon captain Parker saw the potential in Ronnie and took him to England and Wimbledon's Plough Lane.

Ronnie says: 'At my first meeting I was naturally in the second half. I had two meetings in the second half. During the practice sessions they were clocking me all the time and the next thing Dicky Harris was dropped and I took his place as reserve. I had another two weeks at reserve then I was moved up into the team. They made me number two as partner to Norman Parker, and riding with Norman was really terrific because riding with him I really and truly learned how to ride as far as English tracks were concerned.'

At first Ronnie rode for Australia internationally, but there came a time when he was forced to choose between representing Australia or New Zealand which was his home. He said: 'The first couple of years when I rode in England I got picked for Australia and then we started a New Zealand team and the Control Board said I had to make a decision. Which wasn't really hard because I live in New Zealand. Australia played merry hell of course.'

When Ronnie was able to ride for Australia and New Zealand, there was plenty of money to be earned. But for him, it was not about money.

He said: 'Everything, as far as I'm concerned, with speedway these days is about money, nothing but money. And I can't see that any of those guys I read about get any pleasure at it. They are racing but they've got pound notes waiving in front of their noses.'

One of the things that Ronnie thought long and hard about while he was getting well was that throughout his riding career he really had been a one-club man. Wimbledon.

He said: 'I used to curse myself for being such a fool as to stay at Wimbledon all the time. I had such fantastic offers to transfer. But I loved that team. It had the most fabulous team spirit. I loved the supporters. I married a Wimbledon girl, my daughters were born in Wimbledon. Wimbledon was my life. But I used to sit there and think I was a bloody fool not to move.

'Then something like this happens and the supporters all club together to raise that money to bring me here just to look at the place. I wasn't a bloody fool. Definitely not a fool. Money is not everything.

'You see, I'm fundamentally shy. I've never talked much, even to my wife. I've always been that way. It's just that I hate to make a fool of myself. I get embarrassed easily. But if I hadn't been the way I am I may have made a lot more money out of speedway. Maybe a lot of enemies too, but a lot more money. My nature is also one of the reasons why I could never ride unfairly against anyone.'

A very good book was published in 1976 about Ronnie Moore. It was written by New Zealand journalist Rod Dew. In it Dew is at pains to point out that Ronnie was a true gentleman of the track. He would always prefer to outride an opponent than employ unfair tactics.

Above left: The first World Championship in 1954. An earlier broken knee convinced him that on the night he had no chance and because of that he was relaxed and 'the next thing I knew I'd won five races'. Giving the trophy, Charles Eade, Editor of the Sunday Dispatch.

Above right: Family Man. Ronnie with twins Kim, left, and Lea trying to work out who has the biggest Easter egg.

But I wondered: was there never a time when he was tempted? 'Yes,' said Ronnie, 'two or three times. Usually if there had been an incident on the track I would have words with whoever it was back in the pits and we would be friends afterwards.

'It was driven home to me the very first day I was in England. Norman Parker was God to me. He brought me to England and he was captain of Wimbledon. He was telling me how to ride the track – flat out. He used to tell me to ride every track flat out.

'But there was another rider there. A very big name who rode for Wembley. He started teaching me how to do things, and I thought it was fantastic coming from someone who rode for the opposition.'

But when Ronnie got going and they faced each other before the public, the man he thought was his benefactor put him into the fence twice and across the centre green once. Ronnie said: 'I wanted to get him. I was really nasty about it. I told him I'd get him too. And I did, I had him across the centre green at Wembley, not into the fence.

'After that we agreed we were quits. I told him that if we continued the feud he might get me ten more times, but sooner or later I would get him. We came to a gentleman's agreement that there would be no more, and there never was in all the time we rode against each other. At the time I was still a kid – learning. I used to bang into people, but not deliberately. I'd go underneath them because they were going too slow.'

Obviously he was learning fast and, he said: 'Certain people looked down on me, mainly I think because I wasn't one of The Clan. I wasn't one of the established guys.' That was the attitude of the top stars to the brash young man who had the temerity to challenge their position at the top of the game.

After he and the Wembley rider had resolved their feud, and he was eventually accepted Ronnie said: 'They laid off me and I laid off them. It was definitely a closed shop at that particular time. You had to be up in that top group or out!'

There were rumours in the sport at the time that he was threatened. He said: 'I suppose I can mention names. I was sitting in the New Cross pits one night. Norman Parker was on one side and Jack Parker was on the other side. Jack leaned across to Norman – ignoring me – and said: "Tell your boy to slow down or I'm going to kill him!"

'They were making it quite hard for me, but being physically threatened didn't bother me. That was it. You had to keep beating them and so long as you beat them cleanly – not hit them or anything like that – then they accepted you into The Clan.

'They actually told me in words that I was accepted. But, because I was accepted and I was in with them, I mustn't go charging into them and knock them off either, but just race and race cleanly, which I was going to do anyway. They would also race cleanly and if I passed them, I passed them. It was like a union and you just accepted it.

'I was diving under people because they were going too slow, and if you dive under people you are going to knock them off every now and again. After that I had to concentrate. Even though they were still going slow.

'I've had quite a few broken bones, but I didn't find out until later that I had a deficiency, so with an average, every day bang I had the chance of breaking something.'

Prompted about the big names who were around the sport during his era he had this to say about them:

GRAHAM WARREN: 'The Blond Bombshell. A lot of people were getting close and he was an obvious one, everyone had odds on him winning *(the World Championship)* . . . but nothing on the big night. And I think that was what affected a lot of these guys, on the big night they were trying too hard.'

FREDDIE WILLIAMS (World Champion 1950 and 1953): It was generally acknowledged that Freddie had a home advantage at Wembley. Ronnie said: 'He was a good World Champion. OK he had a home advantage, but that was immaterial. He was a Welshman and he used to do funny things just to save money. He used to amaze me at times, he'd use second hand parts sometimes but the damn things used to keep going.'

Below left: Graham Warren. The Blond Bombshell who perhaps tried too hard to win the world title on the big night.

Below right: Freddie Williams. He had home advantage at Wembley, he was World Champion twice but 'used to do funny things just to save money'.

TOMMY PRICE (World Champion 1949): 'Tommy, he was a real pro. A pro in those days wasn't liked by any of the other riders. It's hard to explain, but he had a funny attitude which didn't go down well with other riders. He was a dedicated man. I think he was also too dedicated and because of it things didn't work out too good.

'It was borderline whether he could have won a second World Championship. He was good at getting out of the gate. Personally when I first flew into England he was the World Champion. Terrific. He actually told me on my first practice at Wimbledon how to get round the corners. I thought he was a mighty man. But a few weeks later he put me over the fence at Wimbledon.

'He put me off the track three more times over the next three months until I finally got him across the centre green at Wembley. That's when we called a truce. I looked upon him basically as a god as far as speedway was concerned. He was a hard rider, but once he had accepted that I was going to beat him – he could beat me mind you – we got on quite good then.'

Tommy Price. He was 'a real pro – a pro in those days wasn't liked by any of the other riders. I think he was too dedicated . . . it's borderline whether he could have won a second World Championship . . . he put me over the fence at Wimbledon'.

JACK YOUNG (World Champion 1951 and 1952): 'Youngie was just fantastic. As a rider he was mighty. But as a person you couldn't help laughing with him even when you went out to race. He was a terrific fellow. Jack tended to ride outside and wide, and everyone got to know that. But that didn't mean a thing because he'd swap back to the inside and you would be expecting him round there, and he'd swap and the next thing he'd be up the inside of you.

'He'd use his head, he was cagey. He wasn't a dirty rider except for one night at Wembley he put me in the fence and that took all the skin off my knuckles. That made me

Above left: *Jack Young. As a rider 'he was mighty' . . . as a person he was fun, but made Ronnie second in one World Final – 'he took the skin off my knuckles and couldn't stop apologising'.*

Above right: *Jack Parker. 'He was as cagey as hell, he wasn't fast and I lifted him off a couple of times, that's when he threatened to kill me'.*

second in the World Final. But Jack came up to me and he couldn't stop apologising. He knew he'd had me on the fence, but on the big night you've got to do things. It wasn't a real nasty one, but so that I couldn't get past him he just took the skin off my knuckles going up the straight.

'Wembley wasn't a good track for Youngie. He was definitely a big track man. He would have been better *(in World Finals)* at Belle Vue or West Ham. But take New Cross *(a very small track)*, he could belt round there just as easy.'

JACK PARKER: 'He was a man who used his head too. Jack was as cagy as hell in actual fact. He wasn't fast but he could block you and because he wasn't fast I lifted him off a couple of times and that's when he threatened to kill me. He was good, but at that particular time he wasn't capable of being World Champion because of his age. As you get older your reactions slow down and you start to slow down physically too. Jack was starting to feel his age, the same as Norman Parker.'

VIC DUGGAN: 'Vic was a person I didn't know. I'd read about him and it was terrific to actually meet Vic. Once I was established in the team at Wimbledon he would come and talk to me and that was really mighty. He was good. He was the first man to start using cowhorn handlebars and getting your foot way up the front, getting traction going into the corner and turn – especially on the English tracks. He was really terrific. He was so clean and smooth it was lovely to watch him go round.

'I can't understand why he was never World Champion because the way he rode . . . admittedly there again – age. Those pre-war guys came back after the war. They had missed the best time of their lives because of the war. They came back and had to start all over again.'

PETER CRAVEN (World Champion 1955 and 1962): 'Because of his size and because he was English he really clicked. Because of his size he had no weight to pull on the bike and he really did go. He really and truly made an impact. People used to hate racing Peter. You had to go all the time just to stay with him, especially at a place like Manchester. You needed a mighty motor to keep up with him round there.'

OVE FUNDIN (Five times World Champion): 'His strongest point was that if he didn't win a race he was going to kill himself. He was so determined. I'd never seen someone so blinking determined in my life. If I lost a race, I lost a race, it was nothing. But Ove was prepared to put a hammer through his own head if he lost a race.

'He used to walk up and down in the pits before a meeting started and all he was doing was convincing himself he was going to win every blinking race that night. Maybe I should have been as determined as that, but, oh . . . what the hell.

'I've seen him go red in the face before a race and what he was doing was building up his own mind and body to win the race. I used to look at him and think maybe I should start doing something like that, but I never got round to it. But he did put a new perspective into being a fellow rider.'

KEN LeBRETON: 'He was good, real good, but there again I don't think he was really World Champion class either. He was a man who would be up there, he'd got a chance of picking up a third, fourth, something like that. Ken tended to leg-trail a lot and because of that he'd be in the wrong position on the bike.'

BJORN KNUTSSON (World Champion 1965): 'Bjorn was a hard man, a really hard man. All the Swedes were hard. Even in an ordinary everyday race it was as if they were racing for their country. There was no holds barred, with any Swede. They would hit you, but you would hit them as well. There were no hard feelings you just had to get a spurt on with all Swedes and go like heck.'

Above left: *Vic Duggan. 'He was good, it was terrific to actually meet him . . . I can't understand why he was never World Champion'.* Picture courtesy of Mike Kemp.

Above right: *Peter Craven. He made an impact: Peter and Ronnie shake hands before a Golden Helmet Match Race – 'you needed a mighty motor to keep up with him . . .'*

Far left: *Ove Fundin. 'If he didn't win a race he was going to kill himself. He was so determined. I've never seen someone so blinking determined in my life'.*

Left: *Ken LeBreton. 'He was good, real good, but I don't think he was really World Champion class either. He tended to leg-trail a lot'.*

OLE OLSEN (World Champion 1971, 1975, 1978): 'Ole was a little bit quiet to start off with, but Ivan was riding with him and he taught him a hell of a lot. And he was a dedicated man in the end. He was so determined it wasn't true. It didn't matter if his best friend was in the race he was going to do anything to win. Ole was really and truly dedicated.'

IVAN MAUGER (Six times World Champion): 'I don't think there was a pro like him. Because he was so dedicated he did what he did, which was wonderful, but I couldn't have gone so many years like he did as such a professional. I don't think there will be another person as dedicated as Ivan was.

'He told me that when he first came to Wimbledon and couldn't make it I gave him a job on the track staff. He went back to Australia and riding at Adelaide on a Saturday night, he would drive all the way across Australia up to Rockhampton in Queensland, racing there three night later and turning round and driving three days back to Adelaide again and doing that for two years continuously, boy you had to be dedicated. And once he got going he could think of things like that and what he had gone through and think

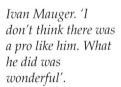

Ivan Mauger. 'I don't think there was a pro like him. What he did was wonderful'.

The World Championship was Ronnie's again in 1959. With him on the Wembley tractor are Brian Crutcher and Olle Nygren.

I'm never going to do that again. He really and truly got stuck in.'

I wondered how it was that a confessed shy man, such as Ronnie, was able to cope with the many occasions encountered by a rider of his calibre, particularly when it came to enormously important events such as World Finals at Wembley.

Ronnie said that his experiences performing on the family Wall Of Death show helped him. He saw lots of 'blood and guts' doing that. He was a great believer in being relaxed on big occasions. Both his world titles were won riding with an injured leg so before the meeting he didn't rate his chances very highly and so was relaxed.

He said: 'I was never a gater, but being relaxed helped me make good starts when it mattered. And I had an infallible system for relaxing myself. When I left the pits, even in a league match, I would say to myself so loud that riders going to the gate with me could hear: "Relax you stupid bastard, relax!" And I would. I'd come off the gate that fraction of a second faster because I was relaxed.'

It was something he taught his pupils at the speedway school he used to run. Young hopefuls would come from all over New Zealand for one of Ronnie's speedway schools. He could improve a rider's lap time by eight seconds. That is eight seconds per lap and not for a four-lap race. He doesn't run the schools now, but the track still bears his name: Moore Park.

One thing he does not appear to have analysed overmuch is his own unique ability. Modestly he puts it down to a belief that some people are born to excel in one particular pursuit. They are naturally gifted. And Ronnie did not use the words 'excel' or 'gifted.'

In addition the idolatry that has been directed at him. If it did find its target there are no visible wounds to show for it; except that he notices things are inclined to come at something less than the recommended retail price it if is known the goods are for a certain Ronnie Moore – and he is grateful for that.

He admits to having two idols of his own – one he cannot now even remember. The other was the late Jim Clark, the World Champion Formula One racing driver.

He was, he said, never desperate to be World Champion himself. If he had been, he might just have turned those three second places of his into wins, and then Ivan, Ove Fundin and Barry Briggs would have had to ride a bit harder.

It never seriously entered his mind that he could be World Champion. He said: 'I looked upon the World Championship as just another meeting. If you won, all well and good, if you didn't, so what? You do think of things like the world title, but the first year I qualified, which was terrific, it was just an honour, especially as you got to ride at Wembley.

'The second year was still good, but the novelty had worn off a little bit. And then, after that, I began to think maybe I could pull one of these things off.

'At my first World Final, with 90,000 people at Wembley yelling, even when you are racing you can hear them and that really and truly does affect you. I was just lucky to get through the meeting in one piece. I finished about ninth *(he finished eleventh – one win and two seconds)* and I was very happy from the point of view of appearing at Wembley

Superfan. Ronnie, as Wimbledon captain, is presented with the League Championship trophy by Mrs Dorothy Charles-Batson.

World Final Wembley 1969. Ronnie had a habit of turning up with an injury, and this time with another specially adapted right boot. But it didn't relax him enough, he finished eleventh. It was his 13th World Final and there was one more to come in 1971, in which he finished eleventh again.

because, in those days, it was the ultimate.'

He confessed he never prepared himself in any special way for a World Final. He said: 'At Wembley we used to have the practice on the Thursday, then we'd go and clean the bikes. It was not the end of the world, it was just another meeting as far as I was concerned.

'In 1954, the first year I did win it, I had broken my knee in Denmark a month before. The surgeon put a metal brace on my leg. I went to the practice and it was hurting. But Freddie Williams came up to me and said: "You're going to win it. I've been clocking everyone and from the start to the pit gates you are the fastest.

'On the night, because of my leg, I thought I had no chance. Because I was relaxed and not tensed up – and I wasn't a very good gater at the best of times – but I made starts and the next thing I knew I'd won five races and won it.

'The next year I was determined to win it but I missed it by one point. So you can't get too screwed up because your muscles are not relaxed enough.

'Then in 1959, I'd broken my right foot. I had a steel plate put on it and I could stand on the right footrest so I thought there's another one gone. But everything clicked and I did five lovely rides and I'd won again.'

Basically, Ronnie Moore the man is about enjoying what he did. He said: 'As long as I had enough money to pay the bills plus enough at the end of the season to get home and then return to England again for the new season, I never worried. As long as I survived. It wasn't a question of putting thousands in the bank. I just didn't have it.

The Boy Wonder is now 84 years old. He has four daughters and is thankful he doesn't have a son because he does not have to face the problem of a son wanting to be a speedway rider. He gave up his motorcycle business when Barry Briggs pointed out to him that he didn't seem happy. And it was a seven day a week job anyway. He knew he had done the right thing when his daughters told him that he had time to talk to them again.

That's when it hit him that speedway, which had given him so much, had also taken much from him. There used to be times when the phone would ring at his home and it

All grown up. Ronnie and the family, from the left are Gina, Lea, Ronnie, Shani and Kim.

would be Ove Fundin calling from Sweden, or France. The conversation usually went like this: 'Hey Ronnie, we're having a party, get on a plane and come over and join us.'

'Heck Ove, it's a two day flight.'

'That's all right Ronnie, get on a plane anyway. We'll keep the party going till you get here.'

When I left Ronnie after our talk, I added a small amount to the end of the tape I'd used to record our conversation. It says: 'Everything anyone has said about Ronnie Moore being a lovely man is true.'

Not long after my original interview was published over a couple of pages of **Speedway Star** *magazine I received a letter from Ronnie. It read:*

Deer John

Just a quick note to say thank you for the article you did on me. I expected to see a couple of lines somewhere, not one that big.

The *Star* arrives here every Tuesday, it is always opened before I get home and this time the kids came rushing out to me, dragged me inside and made me sit down, put the magazine in my lap and told me to read it. I thought of the morning you called round to Mrs Batson's house and my fantastic trip back there.

I have to hop up to the North Island to Palmerston North to run a three day training school in just over a week's time. I don't ask to run these schools, someone always gets in touch and asks: will I? Usually the promoter. But this time it was an ex-speedway rider who would like to see all the local boys put right. It is about the biggest pleasure I get out of speedway now, correcting their faults and putting them on the right track.

I hope you are not shivering over there too much. It was 35 degrees out here today so I'm going to have a shower.

Thanks John, and the family all send their thanks too.

Regards to all, *Ronnie*

SPEEDWAY fans ancient and modern were pleased to be told that Ronnie was back in the bosom of his family after a scare when he had a fall and ended up in hospital.

He wanted it publicly known that, contrary to some reports, he didn't come a cropper off a ladder. He just had a dizzy spell. There was some rib damage and he was kept in hospital for observation. Well he is 84.

Just goes to show, though, that riding speedway is not the only way to get yourself knocked about. In case you are not of the fabulous Ronnie Moore era, stick around. He was literally the boy wonder who took the sport by storm in the early 1950s.

Ronnie graduated from his father's wall of death troupe and was spotted during a New Zealand tour by Wimbledon captain Norman Parker, who took him under his wing at Plough Lane.

Sensationally Ronnie was not only a full international in that first season at the age of 17 (to the irritation of some of the older established stars), but reached the first of his 14 World Finals then as well, going on to win two titles.

He spent a total of 17 seasons at Wimbledon during which he led them to four league championships and numerous other honours, remaining loyal to the Dons even though being offered big money to move by rival clubs. As well as excelling individually he was the perfect captain and team man.

There was a break to go car racing after 1963 until 1969 when he was welcomed back ecstatically and proved to be as good as ever. There was a final stab at it at Coventry in 1974, riding in only two matches before calling it a day in Britain. But he went on riding in New Zealand and Australia until that nasty life-threatening accident in 1975 racing at Jerilderie Park, Newcastle, which really put an end to his glittering career.

***

BEFORE *health problems made Ivan Mauger decide to withdraw from pubic life he* *wrote this appreciation of Ronnie Moore for the 1997/1998 edition of* **Vintage Speedway** **Magazine.**

WE ALL WANTED TO BE LIKE RONNIE
By IVAN MAUGER
Six times World Speedway Champion

MY favourite all-time rider was, of course, Ronnie Moore.

Ronnie was a genuine teenage whizz kid at a time when it was a ten year apprenticeship to become world class. The bikes in those days had spindly frames with plenty of flex, long stroke JAP engines and 22inch rear tyres. The tracks were all deep and you had to learn to control the front wheel before worrying about what the rear was going to do. If you didn't get it right you ended up in the stands.

The racing was obviously slower than it is today, but very close, very hard and very exciting. By the way, the stadiums were full to the brim with this type of racing.

Ronnie is one of the most incredible people ever in speedway. He was the first teenage wonder and the difference with Ronnie was that he genuinely was a wonder. At 17, and in his first year in England, he qualified for the World Final.

Proud moment. Ronnie leading Ivan and demonstrating their perfect partnership.

In the early 1950s he was Barry Briggs's inspiration and later my inspiration and has been that to a succession of other riders. Even in the late 1990s he was still the resident hero at Christchurch with kids whose parents were not even born when he was a teenage idol.

Basically, without Ronnie as the example to follow I am doubtful that Barry or I would have been so ambitious for the world championships as we were. When we were kids in Christchurch Ronnie was an unbelievable hero. I well remember all the kids I rode cycle speedway with wanted to be like Ronnie. We would all cycle down to Aranui speedway early just to watch him arrive, and I don't think any of us took our eyes off him all night.

Many of my proudest moments in speedway were during the times that Ronnie was my partner for New Zealand in the World Pairs. We decided in the pits who was going to take what gate, depending on our opponents. We had a different game plan for the first corner and our understanding was almost telepathic. It was always a great thrill to go down the back straight side by side with Ronnie.

One of my greatest moments in speedway came with winning the world Pairs championship with Ronnie in 1970. Riding with Ronnie in the World Pairs Championship in 1972 also gave me one of my biggest disappointments. Most of the night I had been riding on the outside so Ronnie warned me about a rut right on the inside coming out of the first corner.

I was leading and in my excitement of thinking I was going to win the World Pairs Championship again with my hero, I stopped concentrating on exactly what I was doing. I hit the rut with my rear wheel and crashed heavily breaking bones in both writs and the scaphoid in my right wrist.

Not only was I bruised and battered I was disappointed that I had cost my hero a world championship.

It was pure fate that I was leading when Ronnie crashed at the Newcastle Motordrome Speedway in New South Wales and was the first to reach him. When I got there he had swallowed his tongue and was bleeding heavily from head wounds. The ambulance guys panicked and I had to retrieve his tongue and administer oxygen.

I don't think I could ever do that again. I am not sure how I did it other than perhaps a natural human survival act.

Ronnie has run the junior speedway school at Christchurch since he retired and even today I am constantly amazed at his dedication and patience.

He has been part of my life since I was about 12 years old. I am proud of my association with him, of the World Championships we won, and I am proud to be his friend.

Chapter 4
MOMENT THAT COST A WORLD TITLE

THIS is the split second of action that cost a world title – frozen in time by cameraman Horace Tonge of the old *Daily Graphic* in the days when speedway was important enough for national daily newspapers to assign their photographers to cover the sport.

It is the moment when Vic Duggan struck Bill Longley's machine in a first bend incident at New Cross in 1949. The crash resulted in him high-siding and dislocating a shoulder.

Captain of visiting Harringay, Duggan had dominated world speedway since the end of the war. His 1949 performances – a dozen maximums in the first 21 matches – marked him down as favourite to carry off the ultimate speedway prize that had seemed fittingly to be his by right. The official World Championship was due to be reinstated later that year after a gap lasting a decade.

But, in the first picture, Bill Longley of New Cross got in his way. And, catastrophically, Duggan was injured badly enough to keep him off the track for two months. When he returned the championship qualifying rounds were over.

It was in Heat 5 of the League match between New Cross and Harringay – though one national daily described it as the second Test between England and Australia which had actually taken place at Brimingham *the previous month* when Duggan scored an 18-point maximum. The third Test was scheduled for New Cross a week *after* the accident.

Camerman Tonge's caption material on the back of his photograph stated, dramatically, that it was 'the incident thousands of spectators did not see'. But at least one person did see – New Cross fan Doug West.

Mr West said he had a clear view, and reported: 'Vic and Jimmy Grant were up against Bill Longley and Ray Moore. Bill came from the outside onto the white line where Duggan was. Vic's machine went up something like ten feet and crashed down onto the track, narrowly missing him. He was carried off on a stretcher (in the second picture), obviously in some pain, and we were informed later he had dislocated a shoulder.'

With his injuries strapped up, Vic takes to the microphone (in the third picture) to talk to his faithful Harringay fans

Match reports say Vic was struck by the following Grant as he lay on the track. The injury prevented him from competing in the World Championship qualifying rounds and though he reached the following year's World Final, his towering brilliance was never rewarded with the major prize.

Duggan made his comeback on 12 September, just ten days before the World Final he ought to have graced. Doug West made a special visit to see Vic's reappearance, ironically against New Cross at Harringay.

West, reporting that the stadium gates had to be closed because of the vast crowd gathered to witness the maestro's return, said: 'Vic rode as brilliantly as ever, scoring 11 points out of 12. He declined to ride in the second half because his shoulder was still troubling him. Looking back I realise what a crowd-puller he was. His following was not limited to just the Harringay Racers.'

Chapter 5
CRAFTSMAN AT WORK

THIS rather well turned out chap – formal suit, collar and tie – looking really relaxed, would appear to be more at home in a bank than standing beside a speedway track ready to pounce on the best bits of frantic action.

In reality the image is a rare glimpse of a modest and mysterious craftsman who can only be described as The Godfather Of Speedway Photographers, Mr Wright-Wood.

It all started for him on a coal tip overlooking the old Audenshaw track, Manchester, in March 1928. The dirt-track daredevils captivated him, and In a career spanning a quarter of a century centred on Belle Vue, he became an ace camerman, producing some of speedway's most iconic images.

When riders in the wartime meetings at Hyde Road saw the quality of his amateur snaps they started ordering copies and soon Belle Vue manager Alice Hart gave him a permanent pit pass. A sample of Wright-Wood's photographic quality that brought him to the attention of the riders who took part in Belle Vue's famous wartime meetings can be seen below.

When W-W's predecessor, C.F. Wallace retired W-W bought his collection of 5000 glass plates and negatives. Wallace had captured all the great pioneers: riders of the stature of Sprouts Elder, Billy Lamont and Vic Huxley. Now, original prints with Wallace and Wright-Wood stamps change hands for a great deal of money – if you can find them – and in those days there were no such things as telephoto lenses or motodrive cameras. And flash photography was not allowed. But those natural light vintage images seem to have such a lot of atmosphere.

W-W's favourite subject? Peter Craven. When I was a very young hopeful writer I reported that Ronnie Moore was the youngest World Champion in 1954. I got a phone call from W-W putting me right. Peter Craven, said Wright-Wood, was younger than Ronnie when he won the title a year later. Both were 21, but Peter was younger than Ronnie by 16 months. W-W never let me forget it.

Now, all those precious and priceless archives are being preserved by my colleague John Somerville. And here are some of them . . .

Close wartime action with Norman Parker leading from Ron Johnson, Tommy Price and Les Wotton at one of the 1940-1945 Saturday afternon meetings in Manchester.

Behind the scenes. There were no fancy mechanics to help out, every man had to prepare his own bike before taking to the track, and Norman Parker gives his machine all his concentration.

Below: A true veteran in action during hostilities. Old timer Colin Watson, who started his racing career in 1928, was still thrilling the wartime fans in the Forties.

Below: *Weekend warriors. A team of stupendous talent thrown together by the turbulent times. From Left: Wilf Plant, Bill Longley, Eric Chitty (on bike), Bill Pitcher, Tommy Price, Jack Parker and Wally Lloyd.*

Right: *The first shot in a unique sequence by Wright-Wood of Wembley's Bill Gilbert and his machine parting company at Belle Vue.*

Lower right: *The bike has left Bill well and truly behind and he can only watch helplessly as it heads for the Belle Vue fence with spectators covering their eyes.*

Bottom left: *The bike comes to rest against the fence in a shower of cinders . . . but fortunately stays on the track.*

Bottom right: *While Bill is left to pick himself up and retrieve his wayward machine.*

Wright-Wood's favourite subject: Peter Craven captured in unforgettable, fluid action.

The Wright-Wood study of Morian Hansen.

Caught off guard by Wright-Wood in the Belle Vue pits: Split Waterman.

Chapter 6

SPEEDWAY'S LOST £30,000 TREASURE

THIS magnificent item is the highly prestigious but now long forgotten National Trophy. The *Daily Mail* National Speedway Challenge Trophy to be exact, and its value is somewhere in the region of £30,000, give or take.

It is silver, you see. As far a speedway is concerned it has been lost to the sport for in excess of a half century now. But I know where it is. It is secure in the vaults of the *Daily Mail* newspaper where other such items of treasure trove are kept.

I know how valuable it is because I once persuaded the *Daily Mail*, on whose staff I was at the time, to allow me to film it when I was taking part in a video called *The History Of Speedway: The Pioneer Years*.

If you are ever fortunate enough to see the video what you will not see, just out of camera shot, is a uniformed security guard. I was allowed to touch it, but they had a minder to watch me and make sure I didn't do a runner with it. That's how valuable the *Daily Mail* considers this particular bauble.

The *Daily Mail* sponsored the first National Trophy competition in 1931. It was the speedway equivalent of the FA Cup – every team could take part and there was always the magic prospect of giant-killing dramas. There was also a variety of formats for the various competitions: league matches were over 14 heats, cup matches over 16 heats and National Trophy matches over 18 heats. National Trophy matches were decided by aggregate score over two legs, home and away.

The first winners were Wembley, who beat Stamford Bridge in the final. And the last winners were Oxford in 1964. Belle Vue have most wins, nine.

Probably the most sensational giant-killers were Second Division Birmingham who in 1948 knocked out First Division league leaders West Ham to reach the semi-final. And possibly the most dramatic result was Wimbledon's win in 1953.

Veteran Wimbledon captain Norman Parker had made a comeback after a fractured skull. In the second leg of the final against Wembley at the Empire Stadium the home side steadily pulled back a 28 point deficit. The crunch came in Heat 17, with Parker and the very young and inexperienced Barry Briggs clinching it for the Dons who won by four points.

It was also a storybook ending to a great racing career for Parker. After the meeting he collapsed on the way home and never rode again.

The competition was not continued under the newly-formed British League in 1965 so the trophy was returned to the *Daily Mail*.

Chapter 7
HISTORY MAKERS AT HACKNEY

OPENING night at Hackney Wick. Friday, 3 May, 1935. And tossing the coin before the first heat is track manager Fred Evans. New Cross were the visitors on that historic night, and the riders taking a serious interest in the outcome are, from left, Mick Murphy (Hackney), Joe Francis (New Cross), Ron Johnson (New Cross) and Dicky Case (Hackney).

Case won from Francis and Murphy in a time of 75.11 secs, but New Cross went on to win the National League match very convincingly by 43 points to 29.

The match report observed: 'Hackney Wick's first speedway meeting went off without a hitch. Even some of the established tracks frequently fail to reach the high standard of control which signalised Hackney's entry into competitive speedway racing.'

Star of the show was the home skipper, about whom it was reported: 'Dicky Case who, at the moment, must be one of the best men in the country . . . won each of his four heats comfortably'.

Points to note, the heavy enclosed toe on the steel shoes of Murphy, Johnson and Case, indicating that they trailed their left legs, and the 'Iron Cross' on Johnson's race jacket which was dropped in favour of a Maltese Cross after the war because it brought back unfortunate memories for Londoners of the crosses on the sides of German aircraft during the Blitz.

Chapter 8
ROLL ON . . . THERE'S SOMETHING MISSING

NOW here's an observation test for you, customers. Can you spot the missing item from this picture of a speedway track sited picturesquely among the slag heaps and factory chimneys?

Take a good look because, even though there are riders in mid-race, marks on the track surface where they leaped into action, and a white coated official ready to waive his flag . . . there is something lacking that every speedway track should have.

Got it? Yes it's a starting gate. There isn't one, and that's because the picture was taken long before starting tapes were invented. They used to have rolling starts then. The vintage is 1930 and the location is Leeds.

Known as Fullerton Park on Elland Road, the track was next to the Leeds United football ground. Leeds were late starters. The first meeting took place in 1928 on 13 October – not, you may conclude, an auspicious date to begin a brand new venture, which may account for the rather erratic and less than glorious history of Leeds speedway.

A total of five meetings were held that first year, the last being a Christmas treat for the locals. It was held on Boxing Day. A side was entered in the English Dirt Track League in 1929, but the promotion lasted only that one season. Open meetings were held in 1930 and the star attractions included Frank 'El Diablo Rojo' Varey and the fabulous Lloyd 'Sprouts' Elder. Riders in the 1931 team picture are, from the left: Gordon Byers, Sam Marsland, Frank Charles, Alex Hill, Len Myerscough and Roy Barrowclough.

League racing was tried again for the next two years but the best Leeds could do was to finish runners-up to Belle Vue in the 1931 Northern League which ended in chaos with many unfinished fixtures. The track closed again until 1938 when one final season was raced, but the team finished stone last in Division Two winning a mere two out of 16 matches.

The photograph with riders in action was found in Ham Burrill's scrapbook and was taken on 5 July 1930. Riders are from left: Roy Barrowclough, Ham, Sprouts Elder.

Leeds colours were black and red, the track was nice and big at 420 yards and the stadium capacity was 27,000 - 2,000 in the stands and the rest on the terraces. Attendances that final year totalled 61,776 and the four laps clutch start track record was 80.6 seconds held jointly by Frank Varey and George Greenwood.

The last meeting at Leeds was held, either by accident or design, ten years to the day from the first, on 13 October 1938. It's no use going looking for the track now, you'll find no trace. It is the site of the football club's training ground and an industrial estate.

All action at Fullerton Road. It's Leeds v Leicester Super in 1931 with Frank Charles and Alex Hill leading for the home team, the Lions, against Leicester's Alf Somersby and Fred Wilkinson.

Above left:
Everyone likes to be close to a winner. Here Roger Frogley gets to take away the spoils at Crystal Palace courtesy of a glamorous young lady of the day and a couple of track officials.

Above right: *The Frogleys, Buster and Roger in very early action. Sorry I can't tell from this who is Buster and who is Roger for sure, but my guess is that Roger is on the outside because he was the taller of the two brothers.*

Chapter 9
FIRST OF THE BRIT PACK

DO YOU recall the great days of those 'Good As World Championships' British Finals when what was billed as The Brit Pack annually chased the right to claim to be the country's Number One?

Well, this is the first British Champion. Roger Frogley. But that's not the original British Championship trophy Roger is receiving in the picture.That magnificent timepiece is just the sort of thing meeting winners used to be given at the time, along with canteens of cutlery.

The top domestic honour has had, over the decades – if you will forgive the pun – a rather chequered history. In more modern times it became a sort of Scott Nicholls-Chris Harris benefit, then a Tai Woffinden benefit until he discreetly bowed out to pursue more remunerative activities elsewhere.

No doubt the next magic night at Monmore Green, or Belle Vue, or wherever, will see the Best Of British digging in their steel shoes trying to get their own name etched on the modern trophy which, by the way, was stolen . . . it was the original pre-war World Championship trophy, and to prove it there's a picture of it being held by 1938 World Champion Bluey Wilkinson and another with it in the clutches of Danny King the reigning British Champion.

The official British Championship roll of honour goes back only as far as 1961, which can be regarded as something of a concession because modern speedway commentators appear to consider that the sport was the result of some sort of immaculate conception that took place in 1965 when the big British League came into being.

However, the British Championship really goes back to 1929 when, as a result of the Best Of British in those days being nowhere near as good as the Best Of Australia, the Aussies were given a championship of their own. It fell to England's Roger Frogley (Crystal Palace) and Jack Parker (Coventry) to decide who should wear the British crown at Wimbledon on Monday, October 21, 1929.

Frogley won it. But there was a behind-the-scenes drama in the run up to the final. Frogley wasn't well that day and, as he and his brother Arthur 'Buster' Frogley ran a flying school he decided to take to the air to try and blow away the cobwebs. Roger had a habit of crashing his planes rather regularly, but on the day his therapeutic spin did the trick and he beat Parker.

Speedway racing and flying seem to go together. Roger and Buster, who at one time captained Wembley, popularised aviation among their fellow riders at their Broxbourne flying academy which is close to the Hertfordshire home of today's Speedway Museum and Rye House speedway.

And this is Arthur 'Buster' Frogley in close-up at Crystal Palace. He also had a distinguished track career as captain of Wembley.

From left to right:

Here is the real thing. Roger is British Champion, the first of the Brit Pack in 1929. He is presented with his trophy at Wimbledon after defeating Jack Parker.

Proof that the British Championship Trophy has been 'stolen'. The original is being held by Bluey Wilkinson when he became World Champion in 1938.

And here it is, bang up to date. The latest British Champion Danny King after winning the title in 2016.

The aviators: Roger and Buster at their Broxbourne air academy with a line-up of contemporary top international speedway stars they taught to be pilots. From the left they are: Frank Arthur, Wal Phillips in a spectacular, to say the least, set of plus-fours, Jack Ormston, Roger Frogley, Buster Frogley, Lionel Van Praag and Wally Kilmister.

Chapter 10
THE BOY RACER WHO GREW UP TO BE JUST LIKE HIS DAD

OR...THE HOT HAT CLAN

YOU know how these days, when football teams take to the field they are accompanied by youngsters in full playing kit? Well, in – and I know you'll forgive me for saying this – *The Good Old Days*, the same sort of thing used to happen in speedway.

Here is the proof.

It is of no consequence that the young man in the picture is between two of the sport's most enduring icons, in this instance he and his mini-bike are the stars of the show.

We'll get the icons out of the way first. On the left, 'Broadside' Vic Huxley, one of the original Australian pioneers who, when the picture was taken – in the early thirties – was captain of his country and Wimbledon.

On the right Colin Watson, astride his distinctive JAP bike with the famous baloon tank. Colin was captain of England and Wembley, where the picture was taken. It is purely incidental that Huxley and Watson were nominated to race in 1931 for what was then described as the 'World's Championship', duly won by Huxley and swiftly downgraded to a British Championship because there had been no qualifying system.

The boy racer, now nearing 90, is Ian Hoskins, who got his job as mascot to the

Wembley and West Ham teams because – you will no doubt be surprised to learn – his father, the great Johnnie S. Hoskins, was the manager at both tracks at different times in the Thirties.

Young Ian always appeared in red leathers – how modern is that?

He was, as might be expected, born into speedway in West Maitland, Australia, where Dad staged what is recognised as the first speedway meeting as we know it.

Of course he grew up to be a showman like his illustrious father, and his hat was incinerated many times. A man of many talents, Ian promoted not only speedway in Scotland, Spain and Africa, but also ice shows, managing cinemas and he treaded the boards as an actor.

He says: 'My biggest stunt was to sign up a yogi named Kitao to help Glasgow Tigers beat Birmingham. We won at home as he lay on his bed of nails in the centre of the arena.'

And of course the family hat-burning tradition continued when his riders set ablaze numerous items of his headgear to amuse the fans in the meeting intervals. An example of one such conflagration can be seen taking place at Edinburgh.

Ian saw war service in the RAF and later was with the Rolls-Royce aero-engine company. Unable to get on with the notorious Mugabe regime during his time in Zimbabwe, he now lives in New Zealand and contributes regular speedway anecdotes to a variety of publications.

Chapter 11
DAREDEVIL ALMA

THE AMAZING LADY ALSO KNOWN AS HELL'S GRANNY

Glamour girl. The amazing Alma in full riding kit, complete with shiny boots, and ready to attract the thrill-seeking crowds.

YES, they called her Hell's Granny. That was when she had matured a bit. In her considerably attractive and glamorous youth they called her Daredevil Alma.

Her married name was Mrs. Alma Skinner, the wife of Hector 'Skid' Skinner, and together they took their crowd-pulling spectacular Wall Of Death act around Europe's fairgrounds during the 1920s and 1930s.

Skid also found fame when, as a dirt-track pioneer in speedway's very early days, he rode for Glasgow White City.

In her twenties Alma rode powerful Indian motor-cycles on the Wall and, to remind her of their star-studded career, has all her and Skid's hair-raising exploits recorded in huge scrapbooks along with a collection of cherished international posters.

She began working as a cashier at a Butlin's holiday camp at Skegness in 1929 but, to supplement her £1 a week wages, she volunteered to try the Wall Of Death.

She recalled: 'I had never even sat on a motorbike before. My mother would have been horrified if she had known. But I had always been a bit daring – though bashful.'

She wasn't deterred when one of her colleagues also volunteered to have a go on the Wall and ended up in hospital.

'There was still blood on the Wall when I started,' said Alma. 'But I decided I would still have a go and, within a week, I could ride it properly.'

From Butlin's she joined a touring show and travelled throughout Europe. Her act

Double act. Look – no hands (and no crash helmets) – Mr and Mrs Skinner draw applause from the watching crowds with their death-defying skill.

Above left: *You had to put on a show. Skid and Alma, the daring couple beside the powerful machine on which they used to ride the Wall.*

Above right: *Solo turn. Alma rides close to the top of the wall from where she could snatch ten shilling notes held out by the spectators.*

included riding side-saddle and swerving her bike without holding the handlebars. She thrilled the Continental crowds.

Eventually she and Skid met in Copenhagen and she joined his Wall Of Death show. Alma explained: 'He had a lion cub and was planning to take it round the Wall in a sidecar . . . but it died.

'The Wall Of Death is a funny feeling. The forces on you are very strange. I used to be able to ride to the top of the Wall and snatch ten shilling notes held out by spectators. When I think about it now, I wonder how I ever did it.'

The war years ended the couple's daring lifestyle and they returned to Skid's native Hellaby on the outskirts of Rotherham in Yorkshire and their haulage business.

Then, in 1944, Skid was killed in a tragic shooting accident. While out rabbit hunting at a local farm his gun went off accidentally. He was 39. It was a double tragedy for Alma whose brother was killed shortly before in a wartime flying bomb attack.

Roll up, roll up. The crowds, including children, who used to queue in their thousands to see Skid and Alma in action – the numbers even attracting an opportunist flower seller plying her wares in the bottom right hand corner of the picture.

Recalling her motorcycling days Alma recalled: 'Road bikes don't appeal to me. I think they are dangerous. I once went for a spin on Skid's Norton 500 and couldn't turn it round. And once I rode into a tramline, couldn't get out, and had to carry on all the way to Rotherham.'

After the war Alma never returned to the saddle but she did make an appearance at Sheffield speedway's 50th anniversary celebrations.

The tragic ending. A contemporary newspaper report dated December 1944 on how Skid met his untimely death.

Above: *Skid the speedway star astride his Dirt-Track Douglas.*

Below: *Not a roaring success: Skid with the lion cub he planned to take with him on the Wall in a sidecar . . . but it died before he could.*

"SKID" SKINNER KILLED.

Famous "Wall" and Speedway Rider.

Hector "Skid" Skinner, of Hellaby, near Rotherham, the well-known Showland Wall of Death rider, died recently in the John Coupland Hospital, Gainsborough, as a result of a shooting accident while rabbiting at a local farm.

In an attempt to save his life his right leg was amputated, but this proved unavailing and he passed away the same day.

"Skid" Skinner, who was 39 years of age, was one of the first riders in the Sheffield district to take up dirt-track riding and appeared at speedway races in the city. In Showland he was in partnership with his wife, Mrs. Alma Skinner ("Dare-Devil Alma") and his brother-in-law, Ernest Maurice Morley, in a Wall of Death presentation.

It will be recalled that Morley, who was a lance-corporal in the R. E. M. E. and had seen over four years service, was killed by a flying bomb in the South of England

Alma the Daredevil Granny. Still smiling and holding one of the posters that publicised the Wall Of Death escapades she took part in with Skid. She doesn't quite get top billing but spectators are invited to witness their 'latest sensational act'.

Chapter 12
FIREMAN SAVE MY BIKE !

THE captain of the most unfashionable team in the whole history of speedway racing, Wombwell, was Len Tupling. Or, Tearaway Tup as he became known. He really preferred Lord Tup, but all you really need to know is that Lord Tup was a character. Ee by gum he was.

Wombwell (pronounced Wum-well) is a sooty town near Barnsley in South Yorkhire. The side was among the original founders of the brave new speedway world of the Third Division in 1947. The Colliers, as they were known, never finished above next to bottom of the league and disappeared without trace before the start of the 1949 season. The only team to finish below them was Plymouth.

Lord Tup learned his trade pre-war in hill climbs – he was once Yorkshire hill climb champion. He rode for Birmingham in 1937 and later for Newcastle and the Middlesbrough team that won the 1946 Northern League (Second Division) championship.

He was given the captaincy of Wombwell in 1947 but, true to his personality, he was so disgusted with his 1948 form that he stepped down in favour of Harwood Pike.

Lord Tup was not the only colourful Collier. There was also Gerry Williams, and Lord Tup loved to tell this tale about his team mate.

According to him: 'Gerry was a most popular rider, a graceful leg-trailer, though he never stopped on his bike for very long. He lived in London and rode only for the fun of it. He was a wonderful spiv. A very likeable lad, especially with the girls.

'He used to hire the Wombwell track spare for £5 a meeting. It was a brute to ride and didn't have much power. One Wednesday I went to the track and found Gerry cleaning the bike. He had a bowl of petrol with which he was washing it down.

'I was talking to him about what a rotten bike it was when he said: "This is what this wants." He stood away from it and threw a lighted match into the petrol.

'Well, imagine what happened. I looked around for a fire extinguisher, but there wasn't one so I asked where the telephone was so that I could call the fire brigade. Gerry said: "Don't phone yet, wait until the bloody thing gets burned up."

'By this time a few pieces of the grandstand had started burning. In the end I got the fire brigade there and as they went in under the stand Gerry was trying to put out the flames with an old coat shouting: "Save it! Save it! Save my favourite bike!"

'Well, no real harm was done to the stand but the bike was burned out. The club, I suppose, got insurance and Gerry got a decent bike.'

The Colliers in the team line-up 1947 are, from the left: Harwood Pike, Stan Hodson, Len Tupling, Jan Yates, Ken Allick, Bert Thomas, Gerry Williams, Joe Mitchell

Chapter 13
THE IMPOSSIBLE DREAM

ALL schoolboys have their idols – particularly sporting ones – and former West Ham, Sheffield, Wigan, Fleetwood and Walthamstow star Dick Geary certainly had his.

He recalled that 'in my urchin days before the war my hero was Lionel Van Praag'. It seemed to the impressionable young Geary that glamour surrounded Van Praag and not only because he was then the captain of Wembley Lions and the Australian Test team.

'It was,' said Dick, 'the name: Van Praag. It was a great name for a speedway rider.' To the star-struck young man it also had the subtle suggestion of the swashbuckling adventurer about it.

'I had of course always admired Lionel as a rider,' said Dick. 'On those Thursday evenings when I wandered down to Wembley Stadium it was always Van Praag I watched more closely than any of the other riders.

'His masterly skill and unruffled calm completely fired my imagination, and I'd say to myself: "I wish I was Van Praag." But never for one moment did I ever imagine I would one day crouch at the Wembley starting gate in the same line-up as Lionel.'

The impossible dream finally came true for Dick Geary on Thursday, 31 July, 1947.

Having qualified with Frank Hodgson of Middlsbrough, Frank's team mate Fred 'Kid' Curtis and Glasgow's Will Lowther from the Second Division round of the British Riders Championship – the substitute World Championship – Dick drew a place at the Wembley qualifier.

'I found myself riding at Wembley for the first time,' said Dick. 'I didn't even hope to reach the great Final of course, but in that qualifying round I was up against First Division riders.

'In my second ride, Heat 5, I went to the starting gate with Norman Parker (Wimbledon), Frank Dolan (Harringay) and . . . the idol of my youth, the one and only Lionel Van Praag. As I waited, nerves tingling, for the tapes to fly up I thought of that little schoolboy who had so often watched from the terraces the great Lionel, and now here we were both at the same tapes.

'And that schoolboy, now a Second Division rider from Wigan, was all keyed up to test his skill against his idol.

'Sorry, but I can't tell you that I remember a lot about the actual race. What I do know is that I got away to a good start. The rest of the four laps is just a jumble of pent up emotion. I must have been riding as though my life depended on it.

'There was the roar of the motors, the roar of the vast Wembley crowd and a little voice inside me constantly repeating . . . "Van's in this race . . . Van's in this race".

'I reckon that it was the only occasion that Lionel and I were at Wembley at the same time . . . and I did not see him ride. I finished second to Frank Dolan, Lionel was behind me in third place and Norman Parker finished fourth.

'And that, folks, was my greatest speedway thrill. Not so much that I beat Lionel, but that I had the honour to ride in the same race.'

Chapter 14
THE GLORY BOYS

The professional. Frank demonstrating his skill as a sign writer.

WHEN modern day Redcar Bears fans gather on the terraces of the South Tees Motorsport arena to cheer on their local heroes, do they ever give a nostalgic thought to the the glory days of Middlesbrough?

They might do well to remember the Bears of old who took Teeside to the top of the speedway world. And these are the glory boys who did it; this is the side that won two successive league championships for Middlesbrough – in 1946 and 1947 – when they were members of the old Northern League, the 'second division' of the two sections reformed after the Second World War.

Standing from the left are: Herby King, Bill Wilson, Wilf Plant, Tip Mills, Geoff Godwin, Fred 'Kid' Curtis and Ed 'Crusty' Pye. On the machines are the Hodgson brothers – Jack on the left and Frank on the right.

Key man was captain Frank. He was once described as 'the most notable Second Divison rider in post-war speedway.' Legend had it that he first saw speedway when, jobless, he landed a sign writing job on the old scoreboard at Hackney Wick before the war. He was able to watch the Hackney riders in daily practice and fancied his own chances.

And this is where speedway began for Frank. A Sunday afternoon meeting at the old Dagenham track where young Hodgson honed his riding style on that of pre-war Belle Vue star Bill Kitchen.

He took up riding at the old Dagenham track, modelling his style on Wembley captain Bill Kitchen, and being tutored by the great Herbert 'Dusty' Haigh. In 'Boys' Own' style he helped Hackney to the 1938 Second Division league title.

After RAF war service he went to his native Middlesbrough. The side began 1946 poorly, netting only three points in five matches. But after his return from a severe back injury he transformed the team and they lost only once more, narrowly to Norwich. He led the Bears to two successive Northern League Championships in 1946 and 1947.

Frank was one of four Northern League riders to qualify for the World Chmpionship substitute, the 1946 British Riders Championship Final at Wembley, when he, Norwich's Bert Spencer, Newcastle's Jeff Lloyd and Sheffield's Tommy Allott all mixed it with the National League (First Division) top stars on the big night. As a reward, all four rode for First Division pay rates the following year. Which maybe was why Frank resisted overtures from Wembley to go big time. Only Jeff Lloyd moved up, to New Cross.

The others almost certainly had the same financial philosophy as Frank: why indeed should they move into the highest, tougher, league when they could stay in the lower, not so tough league, and be on mega money? It is said that in 1947 Frank's earnings were probably only narrowly exceeded by the phenomenal Australian Vic Duggan who is reputed to have banked £40,000 in twenty weeks, the equivalent of just over £962,00 in today's money.

The Bears, who ran away with the league title again in 1947 with Frank Hodgson and Wilf Plant topping the section's scorers, killed their golden speedway goose because their fans became fed up with seeing huge home wins. Also, Frank's awesome pay rate drained the club coffers. A promoters' statement announced: 'Attendances averaged only about 6500, and to continue with only that support is an uneconomic proposition.' The team moved, lock stock and all smoking barrels, to Newcastle in 1949 and the following season to Glasgow.

Cheeky chappie. Frank in Newcastle colours as depicted by the great cartoonist Dux.

Jack, a pre-war grass tracker, took up speedway when he was demobbed from the RAF after war service and with brother Frank helped turn Middlsbrough into the formidable side it became.

The fabulous Hodgsons eventually quit racing in 1952 to run a decorating business.

Top left: *Back at Hackney . . . but as captain: Frank, left, ready to take on visiting Norwich, led by the Stars' Australian international/promoter Max Grosskreutz, right and his partner Bill Birtnell. Hackney manager Fred Evans right.*

Top right: *Frank in front of the packed Middlesbrough terraces.*

Middle left: *The Glory Boys. Middlesbrough's 1947 league championship winning side, standing from the left: Herby King, Bill Wilson, Wilf Plant, Tip Mills, Geoff Godwin, Fred 'Kid' Curtis, Ed 'Crusty' Pye. On the machines: Jack Hodgson (left) and Frank (right).*

Bottom left: *Face to face, a meeting of greats. Frank in pitside earnest conversation with Middlesbrough football star George Hardwick, England's first post-war captain.*

BLAZING A TRAIL, THE GALLANT HORACE

BET you didn't know that Horace Albert Burke was a speedway star *and* a decorated war hero.

Trust me. I am not making the name, or any of this, up.

That's him out front ahead of the immaculately turned out Hodgson brothers pairing in the white sweaters emblazoned with those big Ns. A Big N on a white sweater was the Newcastle racing colours in 1949.

Horace Albert Burke? Not a glamorous name, is it? And Horace could never be described as a glamour boy either. Never heard of him? Well, he was better known as Paddy Mills, especially at Norwich where he became a genuine legend among Firs fans.

Why did he adopt the name Paddy Mills? Apparently he had early ambitions to become a boxer, though expressly against his parents' wishes. Whether it was because of their influence or not is unrecorded, but there followed several unsuccessful attempts by Horace/Paddy to carve out a career on the pre-war cinders, one of which was in Leicester, the city where he was born in 1913.

It was not until he came under the considerable influence of 1938 World Champion Bluey Wilkinson, who had given up his world crown to promote at Sheffield in 1939, that Paddy/Horace began to make progress.

Sheffield were in with a good chance of the Division Two league title in 1939 when war broke out and Horace/Paddy, along with lots of others, was drafted into the armed forces. During his war service in the RAF he was decorated with the British Empire Medal which, according to the citation, is awarded for 'meritorious gallantry worthy of recognition by the Crown'. What he did was rescue the crew of a blazing bomber that had crashed.

That's him, a rather bashful looking hero in uniform with admiring fan, before a wartime meeting at Belle Vue.

When all the unpleasantness with the Nazis had died down Paddy/Horace became a real star at Norwich in the Northern (Division Two) League. He rivalled the great Norwich captain Bert Spencer in 1946, taking over top spot in 1947 and 1948.

Horace/Paddy just got better and better. He was so good that in 1949 he was selected as reserve for England in the second Test against Australia at Birmingham (*where he was hated by the local fans*), but a crash at Glasgow a few days before, in which his skull was fractured, ruined his chance of becoming a full international.

He was part of the hugely successful Norwich side of the early 1950s which brought promotion to Division One in 1952. Later there was a brief attachment to Stoke and then promoting at Long Eaton which, at the time, was unlicensed. It brought suspension for him and his riders.

While at Norwich he also ran a decorating business on the side and local cartoons would often show him giving a 'pasting' to the opposition which, on this particular occasion just happened to be the formidable Hodgson brothers, Jack (outside) and Frank.

Chapter 15
THE STARS SHINE AGAIN . . .
FOR ONE NIGHT ONLY

YOU couldn't buy this lot on the open transfer market, or squeeze them within today's points limit. Every one of them is a star Museum Piece in his own right. It is a truly venerable line-up of some of speedway's all-time greats.

The more mature among us will be coming over all unnecessary recalling the names in this unique gathering. It was, by special request, and for one night only. So stick around you modern fans, you might learn something.

The picture was taken at Sheffield's Owlerton Stadium on the occasion of a gathering of what was then known as the Veteran Dirt-Track Riders Association, the prime mover of which was journalist Peter Arnold who is on the extreme right. The type of track lighting in use, and the presence of Ron Johnson, enables us to place the date as 1960 – the great Johnno returned briefly to England that year with Edinburgh. Nine years later Peter Arnold died at the wheel of his car on the way home from a speedway meeting.

It was his idea to form an association of old timers in 1957. He was its first secretary and his lasting legacy is that the organisation still thrives today as the World Speedway Riders Association.

As for the line-up, with the aid of several correspondents, and not least the knowledge of former referee and Sheffield clerk of the course John Whitaker, we can name all but two. They are, from the left:

Ted Bravery (Plymouth, Norwich), Ronnie Cliffe (Wombwell), Wilf Jay (Norwich, Newcastle), Harry Whitfield (Middlesbrough, Wembley), George Greenwood (Middlesbrough, Wembley), Ron Johnson (Crystal Palace, New Cross), Frank Hodgson (Dagenham, Hackney, Middlesbrough), Archie Bingham (?), Tommy Bateman (Sheffield), Don Houghton (Sheffield, Norwich, Fleetwood, Wigan), Roger Wise (Bristol), Len Tupling (Birmingham, Sheffield, Wombwell), *Unknown, Norman Dixon (?), Jack Barnett (High Beech), Pedlar Palmer (Wombwell, Leicester, Long Eaton), Harry Carter (worked in Wembley manager Alec Jackson's JAP shop), *Unknown, Jack Wildblood (?), Phil Bishop (High Beech, Lea Bridge, West Ham), Frank 'El Diablo Rojo' Varey (Belle Vue), Jack 'Bronco' Dixon (Belle Vue, West Ham, Sheffield), Stan Jenkinson (Sheffield machine examiner), Harrison Gill (Belle Vue), Peter Arnold.

*If anyone can fill in the *Unknown blanks, please get in touch.*

TRAGEDY OF THE MAN OF MYSTERY

THESE men are reaching hands across time - four speedway decades, from the late 1920s almost to the 1970s. Why 'almost . . . ?' Let me tell you. It is a story riven with the mask of tragedy.

On the left, Tommy Allott, a dirt track pioneer from way back at Barnsley in 1929. The man with the microphone is Peter Arnold, who could be described as the first International Man Of Mystery.

Tommy's distinguished track career took him from Barnsley to West Ham, Belle Vue, Norwich, Sheffield, Edinburgh and Liverpool. On the way he became, in 1946, one of four Northern League (Division 2) riders to win a place at the Wembley final of the British Riders Championship, along with Bert Spencer (Norwich), Frank Hodgson (Middlesbrough) and Jeff Lloyd (Newcastle). Not bad. It put them on First Division money in 1947.

Peter Arnold, a brilliant journalist, broadcaster and speedway announcer, founded the original Veteran Dirt-Track Riders Association. But – and now it can be revealed – Peter Arnold wasn't his real name. He was really Alan Baxter . . . though no one has yet explained why he chose a pseudonym.

I have the much-prized VDTRA badge with the original legend on it. But the organisation also changed names: becoming the Veteran Speedway Riders Association and now, because the old names were thought to discourage the young guns from joining, it is the World Speedway Riders Association.

Peter/Alan founded the VDTRA with only a few members, but it grew rapidly. The objects of the association – as always – are 'purely social and benevolent' and it has pledged never to interfere with the governance of the sport.

In 1969 Peter/Alan, a widower, was driving home from a meeting at Reading when he had a serious heart attack and his car crashed into an island and lamp standard. He died in hospital a few days before he was due to re-marry on August 27th. But the association he founded has lived on and thrived.

Early annual general meetings used to be held at a pub near Wembley Stadium on the afternoon before World Finals. Those afternoons were always convivial and rowdy affairs, with the likes of veteran stars such as Bill Kitchen (Wembley), Jack Barnett (King's Oak), Jack Parker (Belle Vue), Wal Phillips, (Stamford Bridge), Len Tupling ('Lord Tup' of Wombwell), Bob Lovell (Birmigham), Howdy Byford ()West Ham) and Frank Varey (Belle Vue) contributing to the general mayhem and hilarity.

Now, more sober and sedate AGMs are held during the afternoon of the WSRA Speedway Celebration at the Paradise Wildlife Park, Hertfordshire. Reunions are staged throughout the year from Scotland to Bournemouth to Norwich, together with Spring and Autumn lunches and a golf tournament for what is known as the Rider Cup.

There are independent veterans' associations in Australia and New Zealand, and their old boys are always in touch with each other across the world.

Those who have worn the Presidential chain of office, include Johnnie Hoskins, World Champions Jack Milne, Fred Williams, Ove Fundin, Ronnie Moore and many other illustrious names from the past.

It is a sad fact that, each year, the genuine Old Timers become fewer, and Secretary Peter Sampson is always keen to recruit new members who have been involved in the sport. You can contact him at:

Paradise Wildlife Park, White Stubbs Lane, Broxbourne, Hertfordshire EN10 7QA
Telephone: 01992 476560 (office)
E-Mail ~ peter@pwpark.com

Chapter 16
THE CINDERS

AT THE EMPORIUM OF EXCELLENCE

WHAT a lovely old fashioned word that is. Cinders. It brings back many memories for me of a long, lost and much lamented period in the evolution of speedway racing . . . I crave your indulgence for enjoying a brief moment of sweet nostalgia . . .
That being said, let's get down to the task in hand.

THE wonderful emporium of excellence, Wembley Stadium – the old Wembley Stadium, you understand, the one with those magnificent twin towers, not the garish new monstrosity that's too snooty to have a speedway track – was presided over by its owner Sir Arthur James Elvin who was not only dedicated to winning, but winning in the most honourable, sporting and entertaining way.

The action at every speedway meeting at the Empire Stadium was preceded by the playing of the Lions' famous signature tune, *Entry Of The Gladiators*. And in the speedway Press it earned Elvin the title of Gladiator In Chief.

Sir Arthur's influence on the sport for nigh on 30 magnificent years was incalculable, and his dedication to raising its profile is legendary. Along with team success, Elvin ensured that his 'Ascot of the Speedways', as he insisted Wembley became known, was not short of additional attractions in the name of entertainment.

Team matches were peppered with such diversions as the Wembley Gold Cup, the Wembley Grand Prix, Wembley Cubs versus Spain and the Wembley Junior Championship. On occasions, one of Wembley's biggest stars, Frank Charles, would serenade the interval crowds on his piano accordion.

But probably the most famous and enduring attraction was The Cinders, in which star visiting riders were invited to make attempts on the Wembley one-lap flying start track record.

As London was the Mecca of speedway when Elvin ruled the roost, he used it as a sure fire excuse to book in top names from the other tracks in the metropolis to pack those Empire Stadium's vast terraces.

Success in The Cinders brought a handsome silver trophy and, much later, a plaque. Former promoter and speedway memorabilia collector Allen Trump has sent a picture of two handsome silver Cinders trophies won by top Wembley and England international Harry Riley 'Ginger' Lees, who is pictured in a Test match duel with Frank Arthur at Crystal Palace.

The trophy on the left is engraved: Wembley Speedway, replica of The Cinders (One Lap Flying Start) presented to Ginger Lees who established the fastest time, 19.2 seconds on May 26th 1932. Present holder of record, Colin Watson, time 19.0 seconds.

The one on the right is inscribed: Wembley Speedway, replica of The Cinders (One Lap

Below left: Special attraction. The original Silver Urns containing The Cinders won by Wembley's Ginger Lees in 1932 and 1933.

Below right: Test match duel. Ginger Lees challenging Australia's captain Frank Arthur.

The Wembley programme from 15 May 1947, A Wembley v New Cross league match with The Cinders results that day showing Vic Duggan winning over Ron Johnson, Bill Kitchen and Tommy Price.

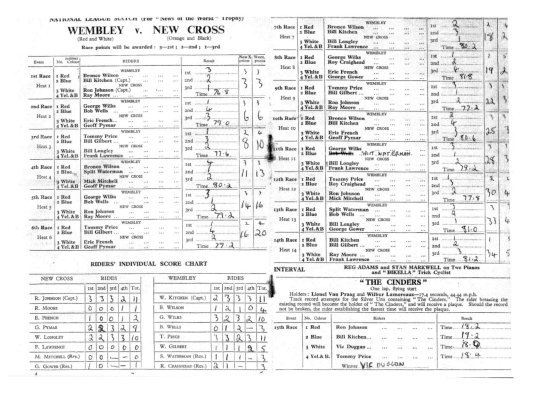

Vic Duggan didn't break the record that day, but did post the fastest time, so he was presented with a plaque.

Double World Champion Fred Williams of Wembley must have broken the record – but we don't know by how much – because he is seen receiving one of the Silver Urns and, just visible on it are the engraved names of previous holders.

Flying Start) presented to H.R. Lees who established the fastest time, 19.4 seconds on May 11th 1933. Present holder of record, Colin Watson, time 19.0 seconds.

'Which begs the question as to why did Ginger get the second replica in 1933 if Colin's original record still stood?' observes Trump. 'I don't know enough about the basis of the trophy to answer that one. It suggests it was awarded each season to the fastest that year.'

Although we are thrown into more confusion when a Wembley v New Cross programme for Thursday, May 15th 1947 shows Vic Duggan as 'the winner' when his time does appear to be 0.2 faster than Ron Johnson's, but certainly slower than the times set by 'holders' Lionel Van Praag and Wilbur Lamoreaux which were 17.4 seconds – though their times must have been set pre-war and the post-war Wembley track must have changed.

Also on the list of holders was Fay Taylour. Elvin began it in the very earliest days of speedway and among the top names to have held The Cinders were: American Ray Tauser, Australia's Max Grosskreutz, England's Jack Ormston and 'Smiling' Jim Kempster, England's first speedway Test captain, George Greenwood, and lots more.

Tauser was the first holder of the record, on 16 May, 1929, with a time of 21 seconds for a single flying lap, which represented a speed of 36.82 mph. Fay was next. She lowered Tauser's time to 20.8 seconds on June 6 with a speed of 37.18 mph. that was, of course, before a slight mishap to a lady rider led Sir Arthur to get female speedway riders banned from the tracks for half a century.

Ginger Lees was one of the great northerners brought to Wembley by then manager Johnnie Hoskins and rode at Manchester White City, Preston, Burnley and Liverpool before joining the Lions. He qualified for the first World Final in 1936 and again in 1937 when he retired.

PS: *You may also have noticed that Elvin believed in giving his customers extra value for money. Billed as interval attractions are Adams and Markwell on two pianos and a trick cyclist . . . Make what you will of the need for the attendance at a speedway meeting of a 'trickcyclist'. And, in case you are interested in the result of the Wembley v New Cross match on May 15th 1947, Wembley won 50 – 34.*

Chapter 17
HARRIS BOMBED

WELL, here's a fine thing . . . something is definitely adrift. It's all a bit of a jigsaw, but if that bike is in the process of being assembled, then our chum in the leather racing suit is definitely on the right track. However, if those handlebars recently separated themselves unbidden from the rest of the machine, then whoever was on board at the time almost certainly had a torrid time of it.

Such moments are all part of life's rich pattern for a speedway rider. In this case it happens to be Dick Harris who, had he thought about it at the time, could have got in decades before the more modern Chris and styled himself as the sport's original Bomber Harris.

However, he appears none the worse for what was indubitably an experience he wouldn't have been anxious to repeat. When his predicament was captured, at Wimbledon around 1949, Dick the daring Don was already a veteran of almost 40, having begun his career with Lea Bridge and Harringay before the war.

That extra padding on his left knee is a giveaway . . . he was a good old fashioned, spectacular leg-trailer. Wimbledon boss Ronnie Greene picked him out of the 1946 pool of talent to fill a second string role behind the likes of wily old Norman Parker, the brilliant Alec Statham and Oliver 'Laughing Boy' Hart. Dick rode in every match for the Dons in the first two post-war seasons.

Selected for the England touring side to visit Australia in 1947-48, he rode in five of that winter's Tests. After five seasons with Wimbledon his form dropped to little more than reserve value, almost certainly because speedway tracks were evolving from deep cinders to slick shale and the leg-trailing style was becoming redundant.

You could say, in this instance, that Harris bombed.

Dick moved from First Division Wimbledon to Third Division Wolverhampton in 1951 then, after a time with non-league Wigan moved to Southern League St Austell in 1952 before retiring.

Chapter 18
THE GOLDEN ARTHUR YENSON GIVEAWAY

YOU won't have heard of Arthur Yenson. He wasn't a World Champion, as far as I know. And, to the best of my knowledge, he was not among the invading Australian daredevil speedway pioneers when they set sail from Australia in 1928 to colonise the world with their exciting new sport and seek fame and their fortunes.

But his smiling face is there amongst the admiring throng in the picture, which is a genuine Museum Piece, taken two years before the dirt track phenomenon began to enthrall the heart of the Empire. This particular gathering took place on 14 November 1926 at the third meeting to be held at the Exhibition Speedway, Brisbane, latterly colloquially known as The Ekka.

Most of what we know about Arthur Yenson is on the back of a small card given away at the time with packets of Morrows Sovereign Biscuits, Chocolates And Confectionery, whose slogan was 'The Best In The Field'. He was No.33 in Series No.2 of Dinkum Sports Speedway Riders – so the term speedway was in common use in Australia even before the sport had been invented in Britain.

Mr Yenson was credited with being 'one of the champions who has clocked wonderful times on small dirt tracks. He has also performed well on big tracks'. In the picture Arthur is the character in riding britches and boots being presented with a Gold Helmet and Sash (speedway was big on awarding Gold Helmets, Golden Gauntlets and accompanying Sashes in those days, along with many other fancy fripperies).

Arthur Yensen

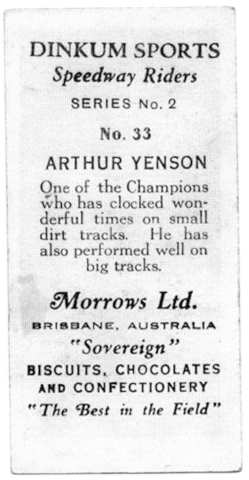

DINKUM SPORTS
Speedway Riders

SERIES No. 2

No. 33

ARTHUR YENSON

One of the Champions who has clocked wonderful times on small dirt tracks. He has also performed well on big tracks.

Morrows Ltd.

BRISBANE, AUSTRALIA

"Sovereign"

BISCUITS, CHOCOLATES AND CONFECTIONERY

"The Best in the Field"

He is standing to the left of that lollipop microphone and the picture was given the title – for fairly obvious reasons – 'Yenson's Golden Helmet'. The incident was recorded by Englishman Lionel Wllls, who was largely responsible for alerting the British motorcycling fraternity to speedway while on a world tour.

Actually, the information on the back of the card is only part of what we know about Arthur Yenson. His usual racing colours were a white top with green stripes and it is understood he 'was an immigrant from Cornwall, who did very well in the early days'. So, maybe the Australians were not really the only ones who could ride a bit.

Thanks to Mr Wills, the photograph is one of the most valuable and rare in the sport's history, for also in the picture to the far left is A.J. Hunting (holding his hat on his shoulder) who, some people insist, did even more for the establishment of the sport in the early days than did Johnnie Hoskins).

Hunting it was who turned up at High Beech in 1928 and put them right about how to prepare a cinder track, then went on to form International Speedways, an organisation which virtually ruled the sport in Britain for a while. Next to him in the white coat is his brother Frank.

There are a number of black armbands on view. They were being worn in memory of Fred Nixon, who was described as 'a popular disciple of speed', yet apparently was somewhat accident-prone. Fred had recently crashed and died after complications set in while he was being treated for what the local newspaper reported as 'a nasty fracture of the leg'.

Arthur's own career also took a downturn in February 1927 when he was involved in a bad smash attempting to leap two fallen opponents. He was hit by his handlebars which badly fractured his jaw. He lived until June 1956 when he died in Sydney.

Peeping from behind the microphone in the picture, mounted in that Douglas machine, is Frank Pearce who Arthur had just beaten, along with Charlie Spinks, in the Golden Helmet Final. Frank and Charlie certainly went on to find international fame if not fortune.

But the enterprising entrepreneur practically hidden on the far right of the picture, with his well filled refreshment tray, could just be about to make a fortune judging by the vast crowd packing the stands. Testament of course to the gold mine both Hunting and Hoskins had stumbled upon.

Chapter 19
HOOTS MON, HURRI-McKEN WAS THE JOKER IN THE ENGLAND PACK

THE joke's on who? It seems Alan 'Whacker' Hunt, centre, and Brian 'The Nipper' Crutcher, on the right, are having a bit of a laugh at the expense of their England team mate Ken 'Hurri-Ken' McKinlay.

John Robert Vickers (Ken) McKinlay was a mere four months younger than speedway racing – born in June 1928. But wait . . . what, you may ask, is a tartan-wearing Scot who was weaned to the sound of bagpipes doing wearing an England race jacket?

Well, if Ken were around today, he would tell you that England needed a helping hand in the first Test series against Sweden in 1956. The selectors had left him out of the opening match at Wembley and the visitors had ridden the socks off the Old Country by winning 49 – 59.

The headline at the time was *'Fundin murders England'* because the flame-haired Ove discovered he loved Wembley and took everyone to the cleaners with an 18 point maximum.

Hurri-Ken's two chums had turned in respectable scores for England. The Nipper playing a captain's role by top scoring with 14 and Hunt backing him up on 12 – but earning the displeasure of the 25,000 home crowd in appearing to live up to his name by trying to whack Sweden's Olle Nygren into the fence.

Even Peter Craven struggled. He didn't score a point – and England complained that they had been forced to ride on new narrow tyres while the Swedes, unbound by British rules, had used the old, wider tyres.

But don't be fooled, said the match reports, 'the Swedes were twice as good as the score suggests'. So Ken was brought in for the second Test at Wimbledon, which turned into a bad tempered, incident packed occasion topped off by Whacker and his partner George White getting into a tangle in the last heat and the Swedes winning by a point. Hurri-Ken scored nine.

It came down to the final showdown at Norwich, where this picture was taken. But the boys don't appear to be fazed at all by the previous acrimonious goings-on and Ken came into his own, top scoring on 17 points. Only the flying Fundin getting the better of him. Nothing went right for the Swedes who ended up having to borrow bikes from England and losing 42 - 66.

Hurri-Ken's distinguished career encompassed him not only riding for England, but captaining England, and also leading Great Britain and Europe . . . Oh, and he did captain his native heath as well, in the days when the Scots could track a full team.

Apart from that there were ten individual titles of one sort and another, including the Australian national championship and some state championships. Ken led West Ham to the first British League title in 1965 and he qualified for twelve World Finals. He came closest in 1956 but fell while leading in his last ride when the win would have put him in a run-off for the World Championship with Ove Fundin.

He wore the colours of Leicester, Coventry, West Ham, Oxford, and Scunthorpe. Who thought up that distinctive nickname? The pretend Scot 'Roaring' John McHoskins when Hurri-Ken was riding for the Old Warhorse at Glasgow.

Chapter 20

HOW RUSSELL PAINE WENT TO SPAIN AND SHED LOADS OF FINANCIAL BLOOD IN THE SAND

THE speedway world of Russell Paine, which began as an ideal dream of sun-kissed bright hopes and self-belief, imploded and plunged him into an abyss of black despair, deep depression and financial disaster.

It took him as far down as it is possible to go. It took him to the brink of suicide and even to contemplating murder.

Should you in any way be of a delicate disposition you would be well advised to look away now. What took Russell Paine from the heights to the apocalyptic depths is for those with a constitution of considerable fortitude.

Russ Paine fell in love with speedway when his parents, regulars at Harringay and Wembley, introduced him to the sport on a visit to Weymouth in 1980. He was then 13 years old. But, as with any ardent impassioned youth of such tender years – wide eyed and clueless – he was vulnerable to having his heart broken by the object of his affections.

It happened. And then . . .

But we should really start at the beginning.

Russell says: 'I vaguely remember seeing speedway on World Of Sport when World Finals were on television, but when I saw speedway for the first time for real it was totally mind blowing. I enjoyed it so much. The next night we went to Poole and it all went on from there.

'We managed to source a bike – at the age of 13 – a two-valve JAWA. We had it from someone who'd got it from John Louis so it knew its way around.'

He then set about tearing up a few local fields 'just to get used to it' and then graduating to the track Bob Humphries built at Milton Keynes and the Saturday afternoon training sessions at Hackney.

Russell Paine was never going to be speedway's World Champion. He entertained no illusions about that. There were junior meetings under the watchful and helpful eye of Kai Neimi and Simon Wigg.

'I was never a natural,' says Russ. 'It was all down to hard work. I did some second halves at Milton Keynes, Arena Essex, Rye House and Hackney. Then in 1985 I signed a junior contract with Arena. The following year I was doubling up at King's Lynn.'

Then it all went pear shaped and Arena didn't offer him a team spot, so he lost interest, sold two of his three bikes and started running a road haulage business.

He eventually answered an advertisement for the Southern Track Riders which led to him joining Rye House in 2000. The next year came a new disaster. Russ crashed and broke a leg badly. He says: 'Came out of plaster. Six months later broke it again at Eastbourne – same leg, same place. It's now full of metal. The consultant said at the time, if I did it again I'd probably lose my foot. So that was the decision to call it a day from racing.'

Unable to stay away though, Russell joined the consortium that ran Wimbledon. There was what he described as 'a big fall-out'. He says: 'There was no one who would make a decision or take any responsibility. It descended into chaos and it got to the point where I just couldn't do it any more.'

He had kept his haulage business going and the idea of taking speedway to Spain came from the fact that his father had been living there for a couple of years.

'When you look at all forms of motorcycling,' says Russell, 'the Spanish are in the top flight. They are naturally gifted on two wheels . . . and a bit mental.'

Russell was well aware of the history of previous attempts to take speedway to Spain – among them the disastrous excursion pre-war by Cliff Parkinson of West Ham and

Wembley, the immediate post war effort by Ted Gibson of Tamworth, Oxford and Plymouth – among others – and the attempts by the flamboyant Hoskins clan, Johnnie and Ian, which collectively left much financial blood in the sand.

But for him and his partner Claire, there was some divorce money and, he confessed bravely: 'It is very rare that you get the opportunity to pioneer something. With the knowledge we had, it could have gone right through to having a Spanish rider in the Grands Prix; a Spanish team. There was no end to the possibilities. By having just one track you could create enough riders for four teams . . . then two tracks. And it would snowball.

'Yes, it was ambitious, but I had a long chat with Ole Olsen and Ole was going to come out and do the basics.'

Determining the right location was not easy. Previous attempts to introduce the sport in Spain had been made in population centres. But Russell said his father knew a few people through living there and a site was chosen between two quite big airports, Alicante and Murcia, and conveniently next to a major motorway. 'Our brief was that it had to be approximately ten acres of flat land,' says Russell. 'There was a lot of head scratching, and then we found the site at Huercal-Overa that was designated for farm use. We told the owners that we would only buy if they arranged the change of use. I never had any desire to be a farmer. They did that, and the local government in Almeria made it just sport and leisure.

'So that was the go-ahead. We paid the money. It was about £65,000 (85,000 Euros). For the land. But they have a fabulous system over there where you declare so much and then . . . er, arrange the other. That did help the situation.

'But, and Claire will kill me for saying this: We were going to the bank to collect £35,000 (47,000 Euros) in cash and I had a briefcase and I said that this was my one chance to open a briefcase that was full of money. So we got to the bank and a man came out with a tiny wad of 500 Euro notes about the thickness of a notebook. And that was it. That ruined my plan.'

With the site all fixed Russell was then faced with the logistical task of getting all his equipment out there. 'One of the main things was to get an architect on board to give plans to people to do the groundwork.

We got involved with this guy who said he was doing this, that and the other and we kicked on. Then we had the police turn up one day with a piece of paper basically saying: Stop, you don't have permission to do anything.

'We took it to the architect who bluffed us a little bit, but really the upshot was that he hadn't done anything he'd said. We got the impression then that the more you shouted and ranted the more you got your stuff done, or you got put to the bottom of the pile and they'd wait till you turned up the next time. He stitched us up, so we told him we were not paying him.

Ready to start work on the project – note the luxurious five-star living accommodation.

'That all set us back a bit. By then we were four or five months in. Then we met someone, an English person who owned a bar near the track, who was happy to help us. I was out there on my own trying to get things done, and he took me under his wing. He had a sidekick, a Belgian called Bart Toppets who was the most amazing guy I've ever met. He could make anything happen, spoke eight languages fluently and got by on five others. He got us onto another project engineer and things started to move on. We got the groundwork done in about six and a half weeks.

'That was another £35,000 to get the land levelled and it had by then cost us in total about £100,000.'

One thing was the material of the land Russell was working on. It was very fine. He was out on the site towards the end of one day when he sank up to his chest. It was exactly like quicksand and he was trapped. He couldn't get out. He says: 'I didn't panic. Very carefully – because I didn't know how much further it would suck me down – I was able to get my hands free and very slowly crawl out on my hands and knees. Otherwise I was gone. It would have been all over. That was a little bit scary.

'It really brought home to me how fine the material was. But once we packed it we discovered it held its moisture, so it was like manna from heaven.

'I saw Ole Olsen at Cardiff in 2006 and the time I spent with him, he was so good. He is my absolute hero, always has been ever since I started in speedway. I got his advice on what he had done at Vojens and I watched how he prepared Cardiff.

'We struggled at first with the drainage, but he told us what to do, what to mix. A lot of it was common sense. When I took my track measurements to Ole we found we were two metres longer than Cardiff, but basically it was a replica of Cardiff.

'I spent some time with Bob Coles the former Exeter star and I remember I was really disappointed when we looked at my measurements because I had wanted it to be a bit bigger. But he stood there and said: "That is absolutely perfect. The last thing you want is big long straights where people can get themselves in a lot of trouble because they'll go through your fence on your bike while they are wearing your kit. When I came round to his way of thinking I realised we'd done the right thing. Bob was my right hand man. He was so knowledgeable and he lived only five minutes up the road. He was absolutely

Top left: The well-wishers turn up. Alan Brett, Bob Coles, Reg Fearman, Bobby Croombs. On the bike, Split Waterman.

Top right: And so do the boots.

Above left: And the bikes.

Above right: And then the rains came… well, when it rains in Spain, it does rain, so Claire goes paddling.

brilliant.'

Russell had already transported a lot of speedway equipment, bikes and kit, to the site. 'We'd been collecting stuff and there was a lot on Ebay. I wouldn't exist if it wasn't for Ebay. We knew there was no Alan Bellham's out there so we knew we were going to have to take as much as we possibly could. Friends gave us stuff. We said: Yes, we'll have it. Anything. I put the word out, people tipped us off. It really was phenomenal.'

There were seven government apartments to appease in Spain and then once the OKs were given they could go ahead. The environment people made three stipulations: Russell had to go to the local council depot and get two big bins because there would be spectators; the water where the bikes were to be washed had to be contained, which he was going to do anyway so that he could put the water back on the track; and he was permitted to use the track only between seven in the morning and eleven at night.

'That was it,' says Russ. 'The only problem was that the licence was valid for just twelve

At least the track now has shape…

… And it looks like a raceable circuit, thanks to the Spanish sun.

Above left: *Which can be just as big a hazard, so Russ makes sure he is protected.*

Above right: *This is just some of the excavation that Russell and Claire had to organise.*

months. But we thought: that's all right, by then we'll have it all sorted.'

But there was a problem with the huge department that looked after part of the land that carried away floodwater. Russ had to wait for month after month while his comparatively little project moved up the priority list of other more massive developments.

So he found himself spending half his time at the local town hall and much of the time with the mayor, who was, says Russell, brilliant. 'He was absolutely fantastic. He was as good as he possibly could be. Claire was working to keep me out there, and when we were about a year into the project we got a call asking us to go into the office. A new man had started and there was this problem.'

It was to do with one of the channels that carried away the floodwater from a nearby district. But there could be no final go-ahead licence until it was officially agreed that Russell's project was not going to interfere with it.

Russell says: 'By this time Dan Lowe, brother of Adam Lowe who rode for King's Lynn, had joined me. He spent about a year with me and to be fair, without him I wouldn't still be alive. We were a brilliant team, we got so much done. We lived in a mobile home on site. Then Dan got really bad food poisoning. He was seriously ill and then I spent the rest of my time out there on my own.

'That was when a guy, a neighbour, decided I was going to be his new best friend. Turned out he was an ex-armed robber from Britain, he'd done ten and a half years for armed robbery. I suppose I was vulnerable because I was living there on my own and it came to light that he was an idiot, no one would give him the time of day out there, and suddenly he saw me as a new ally. He was really a nasty piece of work.

'He actually became a bully. You know: I want you to do this for me. His wife had left him. What he wasn't going to do when he got hold of her. The biggest problem I had, if I was busy he'd just rock up and say: leave that we'll go for a beer. If I said no I've got to get this done, it would be: I'll give you a hand. As soon as that happened, you owed him.

'It sounds really pathetic, and I hate myself for it. It sounds really sad but – when you spend your whole school life being bullied – he made me feel about thirteen again, just by bullying. There was no way out.

'It came to light that he was permanently on cannabis, he was on cocaine . . . I have never seen anyone in my entire life change from laughing and joking to wanting to rip your face off if someone looked at him funny.

'All the time when you are very young and you maybe go out with your mates and have a few drinks I was racing, so I had never been around anyone who was drunk or on drugs. I was so far out of my comfort zone. Things were bad anyway, but then it got really, really bad.

'It all came to a head when he wanted me to lend him £2,000 to get him a cocaine deal. It was: Pay you back in a week, I can turn two grand into six . . . I said: "Can't do that, I don't have any money. I'm out here on borrowed money."

'He just turned and said: "I'll come and I'll get you." He threatened to kill me. As simple as that. And I'm living in the middle of a field.

'I had Morag, one of Claire's friends, living with me for a few days before starting a new job. I think I sat crying for three days. I just couldn't cope and I was struggling with the project as well. It pushed me over the edge. I was suicidal.

'To be honest, if it hadn't been for her being there that weekend . . . we'd been out for

Above left: *And some of the groundwork that went into providing a proper pits area.*

Above right: *Russell enjoys a Spanish lunch at the invitation of some stars of the local Speedway Amigos. From Left: Dan Forsberg, Ove Fundin, Russell, Split Waterman and Bobby Croombs.*

lunch on my road bike. We'd come back and something else had happened, something quite inconsequential. But . . . my bike was there. It would do 175 mph. Whatever you hit at that speed you are going to die. it would have been over there and then.

'How did she stop me? It was purely the fact that she was there. She wouldn't have known what to do or where to go or anything. I suppose I needed someone to talk to. When you are in that bubble of depression and it's getting darker and darker and it's closing in on you, when you are on the edge it can take the slightest thing: you just can't cope.

'Claire was commuting out there every six weeks. She arrived and I literally packed everything up and flew back with her. I was pretty much a mess for about two months. My doctor prescribed some anti-depressants and said: "I suggest that you go back out there and take out an injunction so that man can't come near you."

'Well, how do you enforce that at two o'clock in the morning when you're living in the middle of a field? It's just not going to happen. That made me feel even worse. I had difficulty dealing with people, but I met a friend I used to play football for and he invited me to join in some training. I played in a friendly on the Saturday and within a month I was back in the main team. Football had always been a passion – I was a borderline dwarf goalkeeper – and slowly I got my confidence back.'

It was several months later that Russell was told he had the go-ahead back in Spain. Except for one problem . . . there always seemed to be 'one problem'. The authorities were nervous about his track lights shining onto the nearby motorway. He convinced them that the lights would be facing away from the road and he flew back out again ready to take up where he had left off.

He says: 'There was nothing now that could stop us.

On the way back I dropped in at the site to make sure everything was OK and I noticed that the roof of the container was flapping. Someone had got in, cut a hole in the roof and cut the whole side out and stolen literally everything bar the bikes.

'They had got two bikes out, had a look and obviously thought: What the hell are these? We lost sixty brand new helmets, seventy-five sets of body armour, at least eighty brand new motocross suits that we got through Phil Morris. They had stolen everything that could be used for motocross. We had about twenty pairs of brand new boxed Daytona boots, but they were no good to them because only one speedway boot has a heel. Kevlars were no good either because motocross riders don't wear one-piece suits. We lost about £35,000 worth of stuff. We were not insured. There was no such thing. It's all so vague out there.

'Obviously everything had deteriorated with us not being there and it was going to take about £20,000 to get it all back up to scratch, which we had in place, the money was there.

'All the equipment that had taken months to get together gone . . . well, I took the decision there and then. I spoke to my Dad and Claire and said: "We're done. It's over. That's it." The one saving grace was that they didn't steal the bikes. There were thirty-two bikes in the truck. And everything that wasn't taken was just trashed, it was strewn everywhere. So that was the day when it all went horribly wrong.

'We called the El Guardia and I had a really good conversation with this gun-carrying policeman. He said: "I'll be honest with you, I'll give you a nine out of ten guarantee that whoever did this wasn't Spanish because we don't do that sort of thing. They'd be

Lithuanians, Moroccans, and a lot of Brits who come out here to make loads of money."

'And then he said: "If anyone else comes . . . just kill them, get rid of them. We are not interested. They will probably be here illegally anyway."

'I'd been there six months and I'd been given a licence to kill . . . it was surreal. He told me that there were mine shafts nearby, some of them a mile deep. He said: "Drop someone in there and if they are not dead when you drop them they will be by the time they hit the bottom." '

Russell had actually got to the point where they were good to officially open, and Jan Steachmann was considering taking out the Danish team for practice. Twenty-eight seats had been booked on an EasyJet plane, then local elections got in the way and the mayor decided he couldn't risk losing his job by giving official sanction for the track to operate.

Everything was in place, they had a starting gate, the old Wimbledon safety fence had been bought and was ready to be installed, but it all had to be cancelled.

Russell says: 'It was not just the robbery. There was still this idiot living just up the road – still doing what he does. Supposing we had 2,000 spectators for the novelty value, there would have been 20,000 Euros, suddenly you've got that money sitting around. The bully man was still there. Any moment he could come round and say; "I need you to lend me three-four grand."

'It got to the situation where it was him or us. One of us had to go. There was no way we could have done what we were going to do with him about. You also get to the point where you are so focussed on what we want to achieve. He had to go. He had to disappear. I was lucky in that I had the most amazing friends and all the plans were in place. We were going to kill him.'

Before Russell and his friends could turn assassination squad, the menacing neighbour was put in prison for punching a woman in the face. But by that time, Russell had finally had enough.

Disillusioned, and understandably so, his Spanish speedway dream had reached the chequered flag. He decided to quit for good and return to Britain. But he still owned the land.

'Well,' he said with an ironic chuckle: 'It was perfectly good farming land until somebody put a speedway track in there. But at the end of the day we just left it as it was. We packed all our stuff and shipped it back. The caravan got stolen. But I understand there was some bad flooding there after we left.'

Indeed, people who knew the site have driven past since and reported that there is now no evidence that there was ever a speedway track there.

'Part of me wants to go and see . . . and part of me doesn't,' says Russell. 'It's a bitter sweet feeling. Knowing the effort we put into it and how close we came. But we got so much grief on social media – especially on the Speedway Forum – people saying it was just a gigantic ego-trip. You wouldn't believe it. It was horrific. Apparently we did more harm to speedway than good.

'Because the BBC cameras were there we had to stage a mock opening. There was a "crowd" of 17 people there and the "top riders from around the world" were Bob Coles, two of our Southern Track Riders and me. We had no say how the programme was presented or what the voice over said. People thought it was an absolute joke.

'Apart from the fact that we were doing it all entirely with our own resources. We had no official backing – yet there was a suspicion that there was some . . . shall we say . . . in-fighting within the BSPA. Looking back now, I don't think anyone really wanted to get involved.' With refreshing candour Russell says: 'I'd got no history. I wasn't even a decent speedway rider, only a half-decent junior.'

The entire abortive enterprise had cost Russell a total of £250,000 – a quarter of a million. Now he had to face the stark reality of picking up his life again with Claire back in Britain. They had been living on credit cards, and it has taken eight years to get back into the financial black. Four weeks before last Christmas they finally cleared their debts.

'We have had to put it all down to experience. I'm a firm believer that you're given one life and you've got to live it. Regret something you've done if it didn't work out. Don't regret what you didn't do. We did it and it

Amid all the chaos, two television researchers get the lowdown from the effervescent Split and Alan Brett.

After all the agony and heartbreak of Spain . . . Russell and Claire have launched their highly successful speedway school in Britain and here's the display designed to attract thrill-seeking all-comers.

Below left: It's full-on. Russell's mature clientele are taught the technique of how to ride and slide.

Below right: But it's not all gung-ho. There's a vital matter of theory as well, and Russell instructs a class on the flags they will be shown during a real speedway race that they have to know the meaning of.

didn't work. Anytime you start looking back, that's wasting time when you could be looking forward.

'We are so positive now. We are building up such a good reputation with what we are doing now.'

What Russell and Claire are doing now is becoming known as proprietors of probably the best fully inclusive, all-comers touring speedway experience in the country. They call it their Speedway Ride'N'Slide Dayz. That's for absolute beginners – of any age – and they incorporate their Powerslide School which is the next level and more intensive.

'We had a decision to make. With what we were left with – all the kevlars, and also we had the bikes. I really enjoy the teaching side of things. I've been to training schools run by top riders, international riders, even World Champions and come away thinking: what was that all about? Yet, I was a nobody, and what we have created is mind-blowing, that we can play a part in creating speedway riders. We have several riders who have signed for teams, three of whom had never ridden a speedway bike.

'Three of them took their first rides with us. They are Alec Wright and Darren Manning who both signed for King's Lynn and Danny Ayres who signed for Kent, becoming their Rider Of The Year in his first full season.

'We had to invest more money to start again. Only Olle Nygren was doing it. We wanted to achieve something different and rather than be based somewhere, we are going to be operating at different tracks.

'I was doing some driving, and I took over two lorries. We had a launch at King's Lynn. I contacted everyone. What's really bizarre is that the Elite League tracks: Buster Chapman at King's Lynn, Mick Horton and Coventry, David Hemsley at Leicester, John Cook at Arena, they said: "Yes, come along". The Premier League tracks, they were: Oh no, you're not using our mud . . . no, we're not interested.

'Somerset would have loved us there, but we had to deal with the local council planning people who wanted us to pay £118 because it would have been a planning inquiry. And that's what we were up against. But Glasgow couldn't do enough, we had an amazing day. Really special. All we ask of any track is: let us in, take the rent money and then let us out again. We and our team do everything. It costs £225 for the seven hour day.

'We have been so successful because so much thought has gone into it. It's a speedway experience. It's a buzz. It's a taste of what speedway is about.'

When we concluded our interview I told Russell that I could see his eyes sparkling because he had come through so much and now, over five years, he had at last actually achieved success. He really is an amazing man – a man worthy of admiration.

To contact Russ and Ride' N' Slide, go to:
www.speedwaridenslidedayz.com
or info@speedwayridenslidedayz.com
Telephonbe: 01438 355009
Mobile: 07976 424145

Chapter 21
SHAPING UP

CENTRE green interviewers don't come in that shape at British speedway tracks . . . at least not very often. But – surprise, surprise – they do in California. All the time.

The young woman in question is Margo King, a regular on the mic at the cradle of modern American speedway, Costa Mesa, just outside Los Angeles.

Margo is also a regular interviewer on the marvellous videos produced by Howie 'Hard Hat' Zechner for the Raz Video organisation. If you were at the 1982 World Final, or have a copy of the video of the meeting, you'll have seen her in action.

Talking of World Finals you'll probably be wondering what all this has to do with the other picture, which shows the first three at the end of the 2016 Grands Prix series.

See that chap in the middle? It's the 2016 individual World Champion Gregg Hancock. To the left of him is England's Tai Woffinen who was second and to his right Poland's Bartosz Zmarzlik who was third.

See that little chap in the other picture being interviewed by Ms King? That's also Greg Hancock . . . when he was eleven. He is now 46.

The year is 1981, when Greg's mentor, Bruce Penhall, swept to the first of his two titles in a never to be forgotten World Final, the last to be held at Wembley. Under Bruce's tuition, young Greg was to stand on the World Championship podium for the first time himself 16 years later . . . and then equal his hero's achievement with a second title an astonishing 14 years after that at the age of 41, then again in 2014 at 44 and yet again in 2016 at the age of 46. It makes him America's most successful speedway rider.

How interesting it would be to be able to hear the chat between him and Ms King all those years ago, while his pal Ronnie Correy waited his turn in the limelight.

Margo used to be known as Margo King-Sandona, because she was once married to former star rider the late John 'Sidewinder' Sandona whose ability was up there with Penhall, the Moran brothers, Lance King, John 'Cowboy' Cook, Bobby 'Captain America' Schwartz and of course those other American World Champions Billy Hamill, Sam Ermolenko and Jack Milne.

The Tiger.
Out-psyched by a
mechanical genius.

Opposite, top:
You did what . . . ?
Alec Moseley, holding
the tool of his trade,
delights a gathering of
the Tiger's West Ham
team mates, Eric
Chitty (left), Arthur
Atkinson (centre) and
Ken Brett with the
tale of how he
managed to trick their
captain over his
'misbehaving' bike.

Opposite, bottom:
The Tiger leads his
team to success. The
West Ham league
championship
winning team of
1937. He is on the far
left, then comes
promoter Johnnie
Hoskins, Arthur
Atkinson, Lloyd
Goffe, Charlie Spinks,
Bluey Wilkinson, Ken
Brett, Tommy
Croombs, Bronco
Dixon, Phil Biship
aided by a crutch
following one of his
many crashes, and to
his right Eric Chitty.

Chapter 22
IT'S ALL ABOUT PSYCHOLOGY

OR HOW A TOUCH OF SUBTLE WIZARDRY TRICKED THE TIGER

SPEEDWAY is all about confidence. Or so they say. Speedway is also all about psychology. Two of the finest and best speedway mind game merchants there have ever been were the British Golden Helmet Match Race maestro Jack Parker and the multi-World Champion Ivan Mauger..

Both of them were highly skilled at gaining an advantage by out-psyching their opponents

Not many modern fans will have heard of the name Alec Moseley who, when the sport was very much younger than it is now, was one of the greatest mechanics the sport has ever known.

Alec always believed that the power of psychology was just as potent as his mechanical wizardry.

West Ham and England captain Harold 'Tiger' Stevenson never used to weary of telling one tale of Alec's psychological sleight of hand. Alec used to say: 'You can kid a man into winning. It isn't always the bike that causes problems. Very often it is the rider, but he will never want to admit it.'

At the height of his success in the mid-thirties – Harold at one time held the British Championship title – he told Alec he was concerned about how his machine was handling on the bends, even though he was scoring well.

So Alec arranged to strip down the bike and give it a thorough check. But he could find nothing wrong. The Tiger was riding the following night and again did well, but once again complained to Alec that he wasn't satisfied with the machine's performance.

'Can you please give it another check,' said the Tiger who was riding at Wembley the next night. Alec agreed and took the bike back to his workshop, convinced there was nothing wrong with it.

The next day, before setting off for Wembley, the Tiger went to Alec's workshop to collect the bike. There he found Alec finishing off the machine after apparently carrying out a thorough overhaul. And he noticed that there were signs of heating in two places on the frame.

'So you did find out what the trouble was,' said a triumphant Harold. 'Yes, but it wasn't much,' said Alec, wiping his hands on his customary oily rag. 'The frame was slightly bent in two places. I'm sorry but I haven't had time to paint over the burned spots.'

Unconcerned that his bike looked less than pristine, Harold set off happily for Wembley confident that he had proved his theory that the machine had a fault.

He had a fantastic night at the Empire Stadium and afterwards sought out Alec in the pits to thank him for locating the problem. 'The bike was wonderful and handled like a dream. Thanks a million,' said Harold.

Weeks later at the close of the season, the pair of them were chatting and Alec had a pang of conscience. Placing his arm affectionately round the Tiger's shoulders he said: 'Harold, do you remember that morning in the workshop before the Wembley meeting when I gave your bike that final overhaul?'

'Alec, old boy, I most certainly do,' said the Tiger. 'And a wonderful job you made of it.'

'Do you really think so?' said Alec. 'Absolutely,' said Harold. Did I ever tell you that you are a speedway genius?'

Alec had to own up. 'Well, I've a confession to make' he said. 'I knew very well that there was nothing wrong with that bike,. So I just took a blowlamp and burned off the paint in two places on the frame and let it go at that.'

Harold had the grace to blush when he realised that Alec had out-psyched him.

Chapter 23
HATS OFF TO THE OLD COUNTRY

THE title of this happy snap is 'Oz bound 1932'. And don't they all look pleased with themselves?

It's a bunch of British-based speedway riders waiving farewell to the English winter and getting ready to head for the Australian summer sun. That rather prominent lifeboat is the giveaway, of course.

They are looking pleased with themselves almost certainly because, unlike nowadays when the modern stars of the track can jet off to the other side of the speedway world and be there in a matter of hours – gruelling though the in-flight journey can be – the intrepid band, giving a hats-off salute to The Old Country, is looking forward to a lovely relaxing six week cruise through the tropics aboard a luxury liner, during which they will be able to enjoy all manner of exotic experiences.

Well, I say relaxing. It was not unknown for certain high spirited sporting heroes to enliven such voyages with a variety of mischievous goings-on when they had little better to do during the long, sun-drenched days at sea than sunbathe, chat-up the accompanying young lady passengers – there was no escape for the female on-board ship's company – and generally do what young, fit and healthy daredevil speedway riders do to amuse themselves.

And you have to hand it to this lot, their elegant sartorial turnout does more than justice to the image of a sport that had captured the imagination of the populace over the previous four years, and earned them the same elevated superstar status that footballers enjoy in this day and age.

They were not only sporting heroes, for the times they were very wealthy sporting heroes.

From the far left we have Mr John S. Hoskins, the man universally credited with starting the entire spectacle. Holding his Homburg high is Frank Arthur, skipper of Australia and Stamford Bridge. Next come four Wembley Lions. Striking a casual pose, Norman 'Pansy' Evans, then George Greenwood giving Norman a bit of elbow. He has his hand on the shoulder of Wally Lloyd and behind him, half obscured, Gordon Byers.

Peeping over George Greenwood's shoulder is West Ham's Phil Bishop, and right at the back, half obscured by a raised arm, Les Gregory of Crystal Palace.

The lad in the school cap wondering what all the fuss is about is young Ian Hoskins. Ian found fame first as the mascot at Wembley and West Ham, going on to promote speedway himself in various parts of the world. Ever his father's showman son, he had almost as many of his hats set ablaze by fun-loving speedway riders as did Hoskins senior.

The folks on the right, giving the boys a rousing send-off, are family and friends.

Chapter 24
SOMEONE REALLY OUGHT TO INVENT SOMETHING TO STOP US GETTING SO MESSILY MUCKY

LET'S hazard a guess at what sort of discussion is going on here. When the picture was taken there certainly hadn't been a drought, it looks more like our heroes have been victims of typical speedway weather.

Could it be that Split Waterman (left) is saying to his Harringay team mate Jeff Lloyd (right) and their West Ham chum Wally Green (centre): 'I think it's about time someone invented a device that will stop us getting so messily mucky.'

It has obviously been one of those nasty nights that plague speedway in Britain because the weather can sometimes be so obviously, deviously and disastrously awful. Especially in the summer.

Well, a device *had* been invented that would do away with all that discomfort, some years before. In 1939, by pre-war Harringay stars Norman Parker and Alec Statham. Their cinder guard was remarkably similar to the shale guard which eventually came along to sort out the problem once and for all . . . allegedly . . . and has now been universally adopted.

At the time the Parker-Statham device was shown to the public Norman confessed privately that 'it was completely useless, but it did bring in a lot of publicity'. You can see Norman and Alec putting their invention through its paces on the Harringay track (bottom), and in more detailed close-up (centre). Even though it looks as though it is doing its job, it was never put into general production.

As for our intrepid trio, looking more than a little sorry for themselves – and who could blame them, given the condition they are in – even though they appear to have been at the wrong end of their races, they were all superstars of their day.

Split was World No.2 twice, to Jack Young in 1951 and former Wembley team mate Fred Williams in 1953. Wally was World No.2 in 1950, also to Fred, and in the days of the one-off World Finals had – fascinating fact – the third best average (13.00) behind Bluey Wilkinson (14.50) and Ivan Mauger (13.53) because he rode in only one Final and scored 13 points.

Wally once captained England, but his children wouldn't believe him . . . until I gave him a programme of the event so that he could prove it to them.

Jeff followed his older brother Wally onto the track, captained England and Harringay and reached three World Finals.

Chapter 25
PC... DOING HIS BIT FOR THE ADVANCEMENT OF SPEEDWAY SCIENCE

THIS picture is not what it seems. What it is not is your top speedway star doing his thing to make his bike go its fastest – that is, getting its wheels in line.

What it is, is your top speedway star taking part in a unique experiment . . . testing an electronic photofinish/timing device.

You know how sometimes when the crowd sees a very close finish fans have to wait anxiously, for ages, while the referee decides who gets the verdict? It is noticeable that there are very few dead heats (shared points) these days. Invariably the decision goes one way or the other.

One good reason for this is that there is no electronic photo-finish device available to referees. Former world's number one speedway referee, Tony Steele, confirms:

'It is correct that we have nothing but the naked eye to determine finishing positions, whether there is television or not.

'With television you do have the benefit of a replay, but the camera is not usually on the line and generally at an angle so it is only a guide at best.'

In these days of advanced computerized technology, your guess at the reason why no precision photo-finish device has been developed for speedway is as good as mine.

The rider who was doing his bit for the advancement of speedway scientific technology is Peter Collins, who is quoted as saying he thought nothing could give him a greater thrill than winning the World Championship for England in Poland in 1976.

And this is how he did it. On his way to his third win in Heat 9 with Germany's Egon Muller, Chris Morton and Poland's Edward Jancarz in hot pursuit.

By Royal Appointment. Peter leaving Buckingham Palace after being presented with the MBE for his services to motorcycle racing.

But he confessed that being presented with the most handsome Segrave Trophy ran it very close. Peter says: 'My citation read: "For winning the World Individual Speedway Championship . . . by riding a British Weslake powered motorcycle."

The only other motorcyclist to win the award up to then had been former world road racing champion Geoff Duke. Other recipients have included Sir Malcolm Campbell, Sir Stirling Moss and Sir Jackie Stewart.

The modest Peter said: 'Fancy my name being added to that collection of heroes.' Well, for what it's worth, they could at least have made him up and given him not only an MBE, for which he had to go all the way to Buckingham Palace but, while they were at it, a knighthood wouldn't have been out of place.

Since retiring from the track Peter has survived a stroke and now spends part of every winter in the warmth of Australia, but he still bangs the drum for speedway.

Far left: Thriller in Poland. Peter is chaired by England colleagues Doug Wyer (left) and Chris Morton in front of the massive Polish crowd after his victory in 1976 at Chorzow – and with satisfaction written all over his face.

Left: Running his world title close. Peter after being presented with the magnificent Segrave Trophy for winning the World Championship on a British Weslake powered motorcycle.

Chapter 26
FANS FURIOUS OVER JOHNSON WAR SLUR

RON ACCUSED OF LIVING THE HOLLYWOOD HIGH LIFE

British Champion. Ron reached the pinnacle in 1933 while still with Crystal Palace, winning the title outright after a match with Wimbledon's Claude Rye. Ron 'inherited' the title from Eric Langton of Belle Vue who resigned it after refusing to defend it because if he had done so it would have clashed with his team's home race night. Ron promptly lost to his next challenger, Harold 'Tiger' Stevenson of West Ham.
Picture courtesy of Mike Kemp.

BRITISH fans of New Cross idol Ron Johnson are furious over an allegation that he ducked the war and spent it living the Hollywood high life in Los Angeles.

Leading the charge to have the Johnson name cleared of what could be construed as cowardice is statistician John Warner who writes; 'I have enough evidence to prove the falsity of the description of how Ron spent the war years.'

Calm down Johnson fans, I too have proof to save the reputation of your hero.

The comment that has offended so many of Ron's followers who, even now, are legion, comes in a paragraph from a book called *A History Of Australian Speedway* by journalist Jim Shepherd.

It reads on Page 140: 'There was one conspicuous absentee from service in uniform. Ron Johnson aomehow departed Great Britain for the United States where he spent the war hob-nobbing with Hollywood film stars and generally living in the fast lane. Many fans, and even those close to his family, never forgave Johnson for his rush to live in a then neutral country. But the truth of the matter is that Johnson, whose injuries on speedways would have probably meant he was ineligible for call-up, simply could not bear the thought of spending the war years locked away in a factory.'

Damning indeed .. but the truth?

BOXERS AND SPEEDWAY RIDERS HELP DEPTFORD'S A.R.P.

Well-known boxers and speedway riders are helping with air raid precautions work at Deptford. Photo shows a stretcher party consisting of (left to right) Ron Johnson, the Australian speedway rider of the New Cross team; Tommy Martin, the Deptford heavyweight boxer; Jack Croly, of Millwall (who is regarded as a contender for the Southern area cruiserweight title); and Stafford Barton, officially ranked as the middleweight champion of Jamaica.

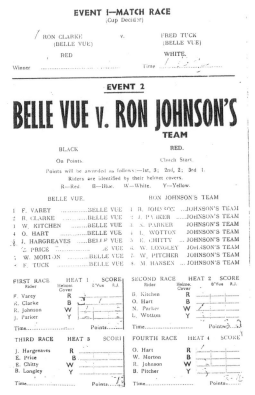

EVENT I—MATCH RACE
(Cup Decider)

RON CLARKE   v.   FRED TUCK
(BELLE VUE)   (BELLE VUE)
RED   WHITE.

Winner ....   Time ....

EVENT 2

BELLE VUE v. RON JOHNSON'S TEAM

BLACK   RED.

On Points.   Clutch Start.

Points will be awarded as follows:—1st, 3; 2nd, 2; 3rd, 1.
Riders are identified by their helmet covers.
R—Red.   B—Blue.   W—White.   Y—Yellow.

BELLE VUE.		RON JOHNSON'S TEAM
1 F. VAREY ....BELLE VUE		1 R. JOHNSON ....JOHNSON'S TEAM
2 R. CLARKE ....BELLE VUE		2 J. PARKER .....JOHNSON'S TEAM
3 W. KITCHEN ....BELLE VUE		3 N. PARKER JOHNSON'S TEAM
4 O. HART ....BELLE VUE		4 L. WOTTON JOHNSON'S TEAM
5 J. HARGREAVES ......BELLE VUE		5 E. CHITTY ... JOHNSON'S TEAM
6 PRICE ....E. VUE		6 W. LONGLEY JOHNSON'S TEAM
7 W. MORTON ....BELLE VUE		7 W. PITCHER JOHNSON'S TEAM
8 F. TUCK ....BELLE VUE		8 M. HANSEN ... JOHNSON'S TEAM

FIRST RACE	HEAT 1	SCORE		SECOND RACE	HEAT 2	SCORE
Rider	Helmet Cover	B'Vue R.J.		Rider	Helmet Cover	B'Vue R.J.
F. Varey	R			B. Kitchen	R	
R. Clarke	B			O. Hart	B	
R. Johnson	W			N. Parker	W	
J. Parker	Y			L. Wotton	Y	
Time............		Points......		Time..........		Points........

THIRD RACE	HEAT 3	SCORE		FOURTH RACE	HEAT 4	SCORE
J. Hargreaves	R			O. Hart	R	
E. Price	B			W. Morton	B	
E. Chitty	W			R. Johnson	W	
B. Longley	Y			B. Pitcher	Y	
Time..............		Points......		Time............		Points........

Far left: Positive proof, if it were needed, that Ron did not escape to the glamour of Hollywood during hostilities. This poor quality picture is taken from a newspaper report that shows Ron, far left, in his Air Raid Warden's uniform with local boxing stars during the London blitz.

Left: And more proof from a section of a wartime Belle Vue programme which clearly shows Ron at the head of an all-star team.

Author Jim Shepherd, it should be pointed out, was a highly respected Australian journalist and historian. Indeed, I knew him well because we were in the same line of speedway business. Jim, who died in 2013 aged 80, was also well known to thousands of Australians outside the speedway world as the managing director of Frew Publications which published *The Phantom* comic magazine since September 1948 – making it the world's longest-running series of *Phantom* comics, and one of the world's oldest, continually published comic magazines.

But his assertion, published in 2003, that Ron Johnson fled to the glamour of Hollywood safe on the other side of the Atlantic has enraged the fans, who numbered many thousands besides the faithful home supporters who cheered him on every Wednesday night as he led the Rangers into action just off the Old Kent Road.

John Warner writes: 'Jim was a highly respected and popular speedway journalist. He was probably led astray by Ron's family in Australia. It is further alleged that the marriage of Ron and his wife Ruby fell apart among the glitter of the celluloid city.

None of the allegations stand scrutiny. Ron rode regularly in the wartime Saturday meetings at Belle Vue winning the 1942 National Trophy and the All England Best Pairs in 1945 with Alec Statham. He worked in a factory in Manchester and wore the uniform of an Air Raid Warden. His marriage to Ruby broke up after his virtually career-ending accident at Wimbledon in 1949.

An incisive interview with Ruby reveals that she met Ron socially before the war. Then, after the war she went to Claremont speedway. 'I went down to the pits,' she said, 'and I said to an official: "Tell that man Johnson someone wants to say hello." He was working on his bike, looked up, saw me, dropped everything, climbed over the fence, grabbed me and picked me up. The next day we were married in the registry office at Perth.

'He was a top speedway rider riding for New Cross. I never discussed with Johnson the money he made. We lived at the Dorchester Hotel, which was probably the best hotel in London, and Ron Johnson knew how to live: his suits were made by

The Minder: Phil 'Tiger' Hart (left) was detailed to 'look after' Ron while they were part of the ENSA speedway team which entertained the Allied troops in occupied Europe just after the war. According to the Tiger: 'When Ron had a few drinks he became rather out of hand' resulting in fights which the Tiger often had to break up.

Captain Ron all smiles and enjoying one of his best seasons. Leading the 1947 New Cross team which won the London Cup.
They are, from the left, Jeff Lloyd, Mick Mitchell, Geoff Pymar, Frank Lawrence, Lionel Van Praag, the 1936 World
Champion, Ron on the bike, Ray Moore, Bill Longley, Eric French and promoter Fred Mockford.

High class. Ron's style was fast and fluid. Master of the overtake, he moves Harringay's Wal Morton off the inside
line to take the lead.

Captain of Australia. Ron (centre) and England captain Jack Parker stand at the New Cross starting area as promoter Fred Mockford tosses a coin for them to decide starting positions. It was the third Test of 1948 in which England just scraped home 57 – 51.

the best tailors and we frequented the top restaurants in London. His bikes were looked after at the track and he travelled around by taxi from track to track. He was idolised by the crowds, always signing autographs at stadiums which were packed. Johnson was the draw card wherever he went.'

We do know that romantic Ron could be a handful, through letters from Birmingham's early post war captain Phil 'Tiger' Hart. One dated 1995 records: 'I probably knew Ron better than anyone. He was a big friend of mine. During the war I lived in Manchester and so did Ron. Belle Vue raced through the war on Saturday nights. I would see him every Saturday with much drinking after the meeting.

'He was employed by a firm in Trafford Park. I remember one night in a pub when a girl was molested by a Canadian soldier. Ron belted the daylights out of him.

'After the war Ron and I were in the ENSA group which raced throughout the British Zone in Germany entertaining the troops. When Ronald had a few drinks he became rather out of hand (you can say that again) and I was made Ron's Minder. On the way home we stayed in Brussels and one night I had gone to bed when the night receptionist rang me and said: "Come quickly Mr Hart, Mr Johnson is strangling the night porter." I rushed downstairs and put a head lock on Ron and pulled him off. I probably saved the porter's life. Ron had hit the porter on the head with a bottle of brandy and there was glass everywhere.'

Phil details various other fights he had to break up, including the one Ron had with Charlie Spinks in Hamburg. Charlie was blamed for the disturbance and was sent home.'

Ruby went on to explain: 'Ron Johnson and I were married in 1949 which was the year of his accident. I remember the night when he was badly injured at Wimbledon. He was in front but came off his bike. A rider was following, hit him and the footrest caught Ron's

Below left: More success. The Evening News *London Cup is presented to Captain Ron in 1947 by a representative of the newspaper with, on the left, Eric French and Fred Mockford in the centre.*

Below right: Mr and Mrs Johnson on celebrity duty. Ron's wife Ruby clutches a bouquet, her reward for presenting the Tom Farndon Trophy to West Ham's Howdy Byford at New Cross in 1948. For once Ron is not in racing leathers and looks the part of the sports star about town. 'He knew how to live,' said Ruby.

head. I could see from where I was that his helmet was torn off. His skull was fractured and he was taken straight away to hospital.

'The head injury did change him. His personality changed. He would get angry for nothing. Ron Johnson had been at the top as a rider and was the best. After this accident, when he fell from the top, he took it badly.'

Ruby said the effect of the injury made him a different man. 'I couldn't live with him any longer so I packed up and left him. I never saw him after that. I never went down to the speedway anymore.'

Ron Johnson eventually returned to Australia and died alone aged 75 in 1983 in his mother's house in Kenwick, Western Australia. Ruby said: 'He died in that house. He had been dead for a week before he was discovered.'

Ruby organised the burial and said: 'The daughters from his first marriage eventually came and took the trophies and whatever there was and disappeared.'

Ron Johnson, lay buried in an unmarked grave for ten years in Karrakatta cemetery in Perth, Western Australia because there was no money for a proper memorial stone.

Half a world away in London, an appeal was launched to honour the Johnson memory, and fans and admirers from all over the world donated more than £2000 for a proper headstone and a trophy to be competed for at a special Ron Johnson memorial meeting at Claremont.

Extracts from the letters from Tiger Hart are by courtesy of Ron's number one fan Bob Buckingham. Other material by courtesy of John Warner.

Left: *The protégé: Ron believed in encouraging youth, and he is with one of those he helped make good, Ray Moore.*

Centre: *Broken man: The despair and disillusion is plain to see in Ron's face as he contemplates the fabulous years when, as Ruby said: 'Ron Johnson had been at the top as a rider and was the best . . . when he fell from the top, he took it badly.'*

Right: *Justice and the final fitting accolade: After a decade lying in an unmarked grave faithful fans from across the world donated enough to provide their hero with this handsome headstone. Former rider Chum Taylor (left), my host in Perth, Western Australia, took me to see it in Karrakatta Cemetery*

AT THE MASTER'S FEET

MANY, marvellous and varied were the legends surrounding the name of one of the most glamorous, stylish and idolized stars in the speedway firmament, former Australian captain Ron Johnson.

You see him here imparting his infinite wisdom to some young men who are only too eager to sit at The Master's feet and listen to him discuss how he acquired over many decades his vast amount of experience.

But you also see him in action in one of his sad last days on the track, doing what he once did brilliantly to the delight of his myriad of adoring fans at Crystal Palace and New Cross.

Sad because, after more than 20 years at the very top, he was the victim of that dreadful crash at Wimbledon in 1949 which left him with serious head injuries and wrecked his career . . . . and, concidentally, his life.

But he couldn't give up the sport that had bestowed upon him, it seemed, unlimited success and an entrée into an elite London upper society – his second wife Ruby said: 'We

Master Class. Ron gathers some young novices eager to learn from him on the infield of the old New Cross stadium.

Doing his bit during the war at Belle Vue. Ron in action at Hyde Road.

Right: *Fallen idol. Ron in what must have been the hated West Ham colours, but the Hammers gave him a chance during one of his disastrous comeback attempts.*

Far right: *Honour bound. Dashing young Derroll 'Spider' Melvin who claimed to have shared Ron's last time on a track at Sheffield in 1962.*

Below left: *The glitz and the glamour have all gone. Ron doing his best for West Ham at Norwich – but the style was nothing like the polished performer of old.*

Below right: *Was this the 'final curtain?' India Rubber Man / King Of Crash Phil Bishop (outside) and Ron. They are here having a torrid confrontation in 1946 when Ron was probably at his very best . . . but it all ended in 1963 in a second half race at New Cross, the scene of so much Johnson achievement. The King Of Crash obligingly crashed and Ron won.*

lived in the Dorchester Hotel, the top hotel in London. He had his suits made at the best tailors and we ate in the best restaurants.'

Over the next decade following that catastrophic crash Ron made a series of desperate and embarrassing comeback attempts. His disastrous time with West Ham was one in 1955.

But an unsolved Johnson legend is the mystery of who was his opponent in his final ride. Australian Derrol 'Spider' Melvin claimed to have had the honour at Sheffield in 1962 in a match race, and 'had to button off to make sure Ron was not defeated in his last ride'.

But a year later there appears to have been a final 'final' appearance, at Ron's beloved New Cross, when he met veteran Phil Bishop in a second half match race. Ron won it because 'India Rubber Man' Bishop, also known as 'The King of Crash', conveniently fell off.

In 1983 the hero of the Old Kent Road thousands was found alone in a house once owned by his mother. He had been dead for a week. Then, for ten years, he lay in a pauper's unmarked grave in Karrakatta cemetery, Perth, Western Australia until a worldwide appeal raised more than £2,000 for a proper headstone and a trophy to be competed for at a special Ron Johnson memorial meeting at the old Claremont track, scene of so many Johnson triumphs.

Practically 100 years after his birth, in 2006, Ron Johnson was voted by the West Australian public their most successful sportsman ever, and a plaque to this effect was placed on his grave.

Chapter 27
BOBBY AND KELLY CLINCH IT

ALLO, Allo, Allo . . . what's all this 'ere then? The couple of chaps in a clinch are the two *and only,* the late Kelly Moran and Bobby 'Boogaloo' Schwartz. Do you think their somewhat barmy goings-on might have been brought on by Southern California's traditional balmy weather?

Or are you just as intrigued as me about what precipitated such a public display of such a mutual admiration society?

Their three chums behind them certainly seem to be highly amused by the situation, and no doubt that sun-drenched, shirt-sleeved crowd in the background are as well . . . but then Americans are like that.

They put on a show, witness an ambitious event they staged not long ago which had the grand name of Monster Energy World Speedway Invitational, showcasing the 'World GB Riders vs America's best'. Whether the line-up really included America's best, Greg Hancock apart, is debatable, but give the Yanks their due, you can't fault their razzmatazz.

And behind it all seemed to be not only a bold move to prove America is capable of staging a Grand Prix in the not too distant future, but also an attempt to recapture the days when the happy-go-lucky guys you see in the picture really were America's best.

They are the American World Team Cup team that finished as bronze medallists in 1983 – from the left Lance King, Rick Miller and Dennis Sigalos. You already know who those two are clowning around in front, and the poignant moment was captured at San Bernadino by ace American photographer Scott Dalosio, who assures me: 'Kelly and Bobby were just fooling about.' Phew, OK. So that clears that up, then.

Oh, and the man in the shirt is George Rich from the American Motorcycle Association (AMA). 'Super nice guy who has since sadly died,' says Scott.

Up until then the World Team Cup, now the World Cup of course, had been dominated by England, Sweden and Denmark, though America had come perilously close in 1980, finishing runners-up to England at Wroclaw in Poland. But by 1982 Americans had really started to rule the speedway world. Bruce Penhall had won his second successive World Championship title – albeit famously and controversially – and he had led his national side to the first US World Team Cup win at London White City over the Danes and the Germans with Kelly and Shawn Moran and Scott Autrey.

It was Surf's Up time for the Stars And Stripes as the US of A rode the crest of the speedway waves. Amazingly enough, one of those riders you see in the picture, who is a two-time World Pairs Champion and twice US National Champion, is still getting it sidewaywith America's best after 29 years.

That's Boogaloo Schwartz, though his name was not listed in the starting line-up for the Monster Energy World Speedway Invitational. More's the pity. If the Monster Energy Invitational PR people'd had any publicity savvy about them at all they'd be posting off a booking to Boogaloo *toot sweet.* Before it's too late. He is now 51.

LARRY THE LEAPING LARRIKIN
. . . OR . . . IF YOU PREFER
THE MOUTH THAT ROARED

AND on or off the track, America's best is sure to grab your attention. Well, here's another name to conjure with: it's Larry *'The Mouth That Roared'* Huffman. Larry in action at Costa Mesa is nothing if not flamboyantly spectacular . . . the singularly sensational leaping

larrikin. Larrikin? That's a person with apparent disregard for convention. A maverick.

Also known as Supermouth, he certainly lives up to his name, as you can see. It's known, around the southern Californian speedway tracks as The Huffman Hop with which, dressed in a tuxedo, he introduces the riders. His unique style of presenting could inject some US-type razzmatazz into a few lack-lustre British speedway meetings.

So to look at him you wouldn't think he has just cheated death, would you? But he has.

He's been battling a problem as bad as any on-track injury. There has been emergency bypass surgery to unblock a main artery. Things were so touch and go that Larry was placed in a medically induced coma for three weeks while calf muscles were removed from his left leg and part of a foot was amputated. His vital internal functions were dying. And so was he.

But after nine additional surgeries he was transferred to a rehabilitation hospital. His surgeon said: 'When I'm done Larry will be able to do The Huffman Hop again.'

Larry said: 'I'm truly blessed. I wouldn't be here now if it wasn't for the care and concern of KC – my wife Kathleen – who is absolutely the best wife in the world. I may be down but I'm not out.'

His career involved a myriad radio, television and movie, shows – he hosted and co-wrote the seminal US motorcycle film *On Any Sunday 11* – and his speedway connection began when Costa Mesa czar Harry Oxley invited him to become the real voice of Orange County at his iconic Los Angeles race track.

'It opened a lot of doors for me and I'll always appreciate what Harry did for me,' says Larry.

Apart from the famous Hop, the tuxedo habit arose, he says, when he asked himself: 'What is the most ridiculous outfit I could wear to a motorcycle dirt track event . . . ?'

And Larry claims European roots. Family legend has it that an ancestor was an armourer for William The Conquerer at the Battle of Hastings and in reward for his faithful service he was given the village of Pangbourne in Berkshire.

Larry lives in Big Bear City, California, from where he operates his pubic relations and announcing business. His talents have earned him membership of the AMA and Trailblazers Halls of Fame, and he is also pictured receiving his award.

Chapter 28
THE DEVIL WHO BECAME AN ANGEL

MODERN fans will be familiar with the race jacket. Yellow with a red devil. The colours of Plymouth's speedway team, which has enjoyed – if that be the proper word – a long and, shall we say, inglorious history.

Modern fans will, presumably, also be familiar with such names as Ben Barker, Ryan Fisher and Cory Gathercole.

They may not be at all familiar with our dashing hero pictured here. Ivan Kessell is the name folks, and he was Plymouth's top scorer in 1947 in a newly formed Third Division. Speedway was on a roll then with millions thronging through the turnstiles. Unfortunately the Devils weren't on a roll. They finished bottom of the league.

But, back in 1932, Plymouth were in the First Division, then the National League . . . am I confusing you? The National League in those days was what we now call the Premiership. And the Devils entertained such illustrious teams as Crystal Palace, Belle Vue and the mighty Wembley.

Yet in spite of top stars of the calibre of Bert Spencer, Bill Clibbert, Eric Collins, Phil 'Tiger' Hart and Ted bravery wearing their colours, they still finished at the foot of the table.

There seems to be no mention of any of this in Plymouth's present website, perhaps because they prefer not to be reminded of such painful memories.

However, Ivan Kessell was something else. There appears to be some confusion about the exact year of his birth – either it was 1916 or 1919, biographers disagree – but he was a Cornishman and an agricultural engineer who met with some grasstrack success as a teenager. One of his main rivals was the spectacular Lloyd 'Cowboy' Goffe who went on to be a World Finalist during a distinguished career with Wimbledon and Harringay.

Young Ivan had speedway trials at Southampton in 1939 and became a protégé of speedway's only Old Etonian, Mike Erskine, who enjoyed a famous reputation as a frame builder when with post-war Wimbledon. His Staride bikes were used by all the big names of the day.

Following second halves at West Ham after the war, Ivan signed for Plymouth and he and Stan Lanfear, with the help of the likes of Charlie Challis, Billy Newell and Vic Gent, held together what was the weakest team in the league – or, if you prefer, the strongest, because they were holding all the others up.

In the process Ivan notched an average of almost 8 points a match which included two full maximums and one paid.

He rode for Plymouth for only three seasons. He then forsook the track, at first to open a successful car dealership. Then, one day, he attended a crusade by the American evangelist Billy Graham . . . and forsook such worldly things to become a Methodist lay preacher.

Ivan went on to form two male voice choirs, and there seems to be no confusion about when he died. It was in 1986. So, at the age of 70, or perhaps 67, the Devil, you might say, became an angel.

Chapter 29
MIRACLE HEALER

NOBBY, THE MAN WHO HAD A SPECIAL RECIPE FOR MENDING SPORTS STARS

SPEEDWAY is a tough old game. And after a hard meeting dicing with danger, and doing your daring best to entertain the fans, a star of the track needs a little TLC.

Gathered here, waiting their turn to enjoy a relaxing bit of attention from our latter day physiotherapist, is what can only be described as a galaxy of famous stars. There are no less than three World Champions – though one is unofficial. The rest are common or garden internationals.

Quite coincidentally every one of these cinder-stained, leather-clad heroes of the track is an Australian so this dressing room drama, it is fairly safe to assume, took place after a hard-fought Test match against the Old Enemy England. And very likely at Wimbledon because the manipulator in the white coat is Nobby Clarke, the Dons' trainer in those days.

The gentleman prone on the treatment table is one of Wimbledon's greatest stars, Victor Nelson Huxley, nominated as holder of the first 'World Championship' to be held in Britain in 1931, which was later downgraded to a British title because there had been no proper qualification process open to all.

The surroundings are rather basic compared with the ultra-modern clinical facilities available to riders now – there are a few bars of soap under the trestle massage table, some odd looking cans and bottles at the back which could contain the liniments kept on hand to ease aches and pains picked up in the course of a meeting, what could be an oxygen administering machine up there next to them, and something that looks like a heat lamp.

None of the assembled company appears to have been in a hurry to use the showers and all of them seem to be in rare good humour – maybe they had won the match. They are, from the left, Jack Sharp of Wimbledon, Dicky Smythe of Harringay and next in line for the slab by the look of it, just behind him Dick Case of Hackney, Lionel Van Praag of

Dressing room drama. A rare galaxy of cinder stained sporting daredevils queue for Nobby Clarke's attention on his treatment table. They are, from the left Jack Sharp, Dicky Smythe, Dick Case (partially hidden), Lionel Van Praag, Bluey Wilkinson and Max Grosskreutz. On the table Vic Huxley.

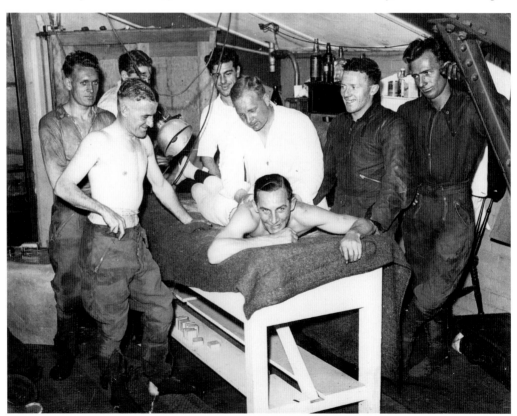

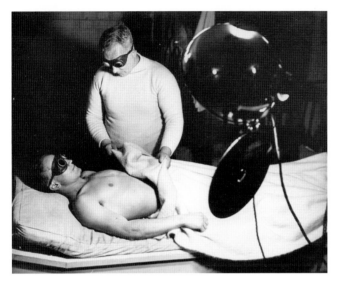

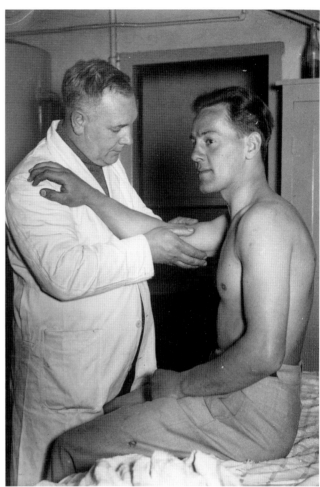

Wembley and the first official World Champion in 1936, Bluey Wilkinson of West Ham, World Champion in 1938, and Max Grosskreutz of Belle Vue, the only one who looks as though he is not exactly relishing the prospect of taking his turn to be pummelled.

It may well have been true, in the words of the 19th century Scottish poet William Edmondstoune Aytoun, that 'fame can never heal', but if you were a famous speedway star and brought your bruises to Nobby Clarke, you could bet that his magic fingers could fix it.

In most of the Wimbledon team photos of the 1930s, Nobby can be seen with the great stars of the Dons. He is the fellow in a white coat and is listed as trainer. Nobby's job was to keep the team fit to race.

So why was Nobby so important to the pre-war Dons and why was he held in such great esteem?

He was certainly one of the foremost sports trainers in the British Isles before the Second World War. Such was his fame in the sporting world that he was rightly called 'the miracle healer'. The Canadian Ice Hockey players went further as they called Nobby "the best trainer in the world".

For more than 30 years he trained athletes of all kinds – jockeys, tennis stars, track runners, swimmers, boxers, wrestlers, footballers, ice hockey teams, ice skaters and, of course, speedway riders – in fact all sorts of sportsmen and women.

He was a gruff voiced cockney, born within the sound of Bow Bells, well built with iron-grey hair. When he barked it would sound like a declaration of war; but that was just his gruff but friendly way. Everyone said that he had a heart of gold. Like all cockneys, he had a great sense of fun and would do his best to keep everyone smiling.

Nobby had worked at the London Hospital and was a staff member of the St John Ambulance Brigade. It was in this capacity he attended the meetings and practice at High Beech in that first season of 1928. At the end of 1929 he moved to Lea Bridge and a year later went to Stamford Bridge. Frank Arthur introduced him to International Speedways Ltd, and he became their permanent trainer in 1931.

Nobby was therefore the first official trainer to be attached to speedway and he then played an important part in the physical condition of the riders.

He was given his own dressing room at Wimbledon which was a replica of Arsenal Football Club's treatment room at the time.

Clockwise from top left:
You could find Nobby everywhere… if you looked hard enough. He is the lurking white coated figure on the right of the entrance to the Belle Vue pits ready to administer his magic to anyone who needed it.

Into action. Nobby giving the embrocation treatment to a stripped off Geoff Pymar for what appears to be a bicep problem.

Next step. A sunray session.

Max's turn on the table. Nobby was justifiably proud of his impressive array of – for the time – modern electrical apparatus.

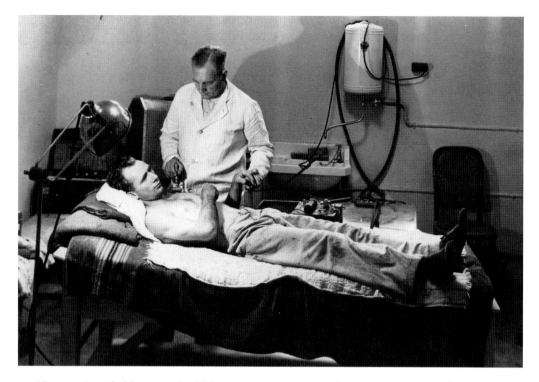

He was justifiably proud of his impressive array of equipment, including the new electrical massage gadget. In all, £600 worth of apparatus was installed (a fortune before the war). This included, infrared rays, radiant heat lamps, Faradic coils and foam baths. One of the most valuable parts of his first aid equipment was an inexpensive child's paintbrush, used to get the cinders out of the rider's eyes.

Nobby had his own embrocation for rubbing muscles. It was made up of equal parts of oil of wintergreen and olive oil. When he had rubbed the muscles sufficiently, he would wipe the surplus off with wadding or cotton tissue. That was important, because the wintergreen could burn painfully if left on the skin.

He had a great passion for the health effects of oranges and would buy them in cases. He also would have a bottle of strong, sweet lemonade that his charges could take a mouthful of from time to time as a stimulant – sugar and lemon juice are full of vitamins and energy.

Nobby's job was to keep the Wimbledon riders in top physical condition and he directs some of them in a keep fit session at Plough Lane.

On away trips, Nobby never believed in taking risks as he had a deep-rooted fear of being unable to procure what he regarded as necessary utensils at away tracks. He always

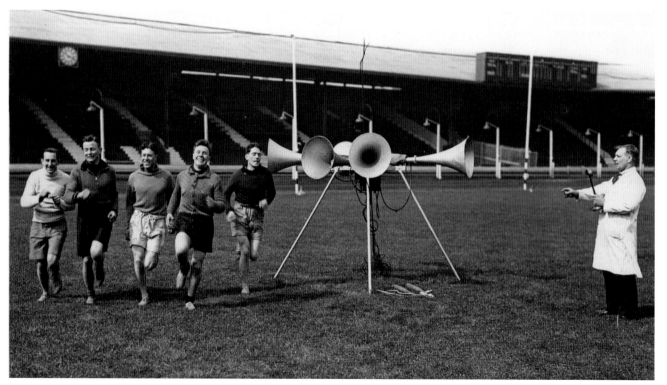

included among his equipment an extremely large bucket and a watering can to match. Just what he did with the watering can no one ever found out.

The great Vic Huxley had so much faith in Nobby that he would never ride, if he could help it, unless Nobby was in the pits. Once, in a Test Match at New Cross, Vic hit the fence, came down and caught his foot in the back wheel. The machine had to be cut away to free him and it was found that two small bones in his foot had been broken. He submitted patiently to an X-ray examination, but after that he would not once see a doctor. He refused point blank to let anyone but Nobby touch him.

Wimbledon, decided to give Vic, their star man, complete rest so he was sent to Cornwall. It was then

arranged for Nobby to go down while Vic's foot was still encased in plaster and treat him for about three weeks to ensure that the bones would knit perfectly.

Each round trip meant a journey of about 500 miles.

Once, when Huxley injured an ankle during the British Open Championship when the score was one each, the deciding race was delayed for about half an hour while Nobby worked on 'Hux' in the dressing room. After Nobby's magic fingers had administered radiant heat and massage treatment Vic went out and won the title.

It was because of Huxley's faith in Nobby that the Wimbledon management agreed to Nobby's appointment as trainer to Huxley's Australian team in 1931. Max Grosskreutz's rapid improvement was due to Nobby's treatment. At the end of the series the Australians presented Nobby with a plaque on which was a golden leg-trailing rider and the national flags of the two countries.

During the 1932 season Vic Huxley formed a scratch team of Australian riders, all of whom were attached to Stamford Bridge and Wimbledon. They called themselves The Kangaroos and rode a total of 20 second half challenge matches at various tracks, winning nineteen and drawing one and, of course, Vic had Nobby as their trainer.

In 1933 West Ham's Bluey Wilkinson had damaged his shoulder in a heavy fall, and on the way to Belle Vue he was worked on by Nobby for practically the whole journey. When they got to Manchester Bluey was in good enough shape to go out and race, practically winning the match for his side.

A clock was presented to Nobby at the last West Ham meeting of the season. Nobby was asked to leave it behind as West Ham boss Johnnie Hoskins hadn't had the time to get it engraved. Nobby's wife, believing that engraving might spoil the clock, decided to take

But then a few get a chance to take a breather. Riders in the picture include Ron Howes, Bill Rogers and Eric Collins behind a less than lethal looking machine . . . maybe Nobby made them all do a bit of pedalling as well.

And here is Nobby's collection of happy looking Dons. Standing: Eric Collins, Gus Kuhn, Wal Phillips, Claude Rye, Wal Morton and Nobby. Sitting: Geoff Pymar, Vic Huxley, Syd Jackson and Jack Sharp.

Nobby the International Man with the Australian team at Belle Vue in 1933. He was Australia's permanent official trainer. On parade are, from the left, Bluey Wilkinson, Ron Johnson, Lionel Van Praag, Jack Sharp, Vic Huxley, manager Arthur Simcock, Norman Pritchard, who was the first editor of Speedway News *magazine, Dicky Case, Max Grosskreutz and Wally Little. Nobby is on the far right and it looks as though he has already been called upon to treat Vic Huxley who has a bandaged chin.*

The pupil. Former star Wimbledon man Wal Phillips, forced into retirement from the track with a leg injury, wanted to qualify as a trainer and became Nobby's assistant at Harringay to be tutored in the tricks of the trainer's trade. They are working on top ice hockey player Joe Beaton.

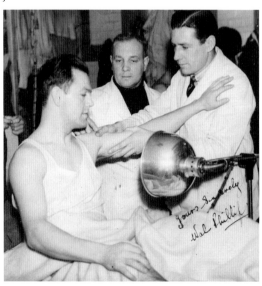

it home as it was. It was certainly a fine clock, some 60 years later it was still keeping the correct time.

There was the time when Nobby was on the train going to a meeting at Plymouth with Frank Arthur who was in some pain from a hand injury. The pain was so bad Frank had decided not to ride. However, during the trip Nobby worked his magic and on arrival at Plymouth, Frank not only rode but be also set a new track record, which stood unbeaten for some years.

Before the war tracks had deep cinders surfaces and, with riders using the leg-trailing style, their bodies took a lot of punishment; enlarged joints through accidental blows and damaged ankles caused by dragging the foot in the deep dirt. These, and the deeper-seated bruises, were dealt with by means of the infrared lamp.

Then there was the common injury to the abductor muscle, when a tendon is torn away from the pelvis through the general jolting and strain from the foot trailing in the cinders. For this Nobby used heat and the Faradic device of applying negative and positive electrodes to the affected part, which helps to build up the damaged muscle.

Wal Phillips had painful memories of this injury. At Plymouth, one night in 1933 he was sandwiched between another rider and the fence. His tendon was completely torn away and Nobby was sent to fetch Wal from hospital by train and ambulance.

In 1934, the quietly spoken, rather shy young Suffolk lad Geoff Pymar joined the Dons. He soon became one of Nobby's most ardent admirers as he adopted a lot of Nobby's recommendation's and followed them to the end of his days.

Nobby's advice must certainly have worked on Geoff, as he was still racing in his 50s and he lived to the great age of 90. In his eighties he was riding a pushbike to his local Golf course at Diss and then playing two rounds of golf before setting off back home on the bike.

During the winters Nobby became involved in ice hockey, working for two years with the Richmond Hawks and the Brighton Tigers. Then, when Harringay opened for the 1936-37 season, he worked with the two Harringay teams, the Greyhounds and Racers. Harringay had excellent training rooms for the players

and Nobby was proud that he had over £200 worth of medical apparatus with which to treat injured players.

The Great Britain ice hockey team won their first and only World Championship in 1936. That same year they also won Olympic Gold and the European title, which were contested at the same tournament in Garmisch, Bavaria. They were the first nation to do so – and Nobby was their trainer.

He also helped Cecilia Colledge who became the British, European and World Ice Dancing Champion.

On top of all this, he was also involved with Metro-Goldwyn Mayer who had a school at which large numbers of young women were taught to be professional dancers for the theatre and cinema.

In the winter of 1936-37 Wal Phillips rode in Australia where he sustained a badly broken leg at the Sydney Showground. He then retired from racing and took over as the non-riding captain of Wimbledon for the 1939 season. He decided to become a qualified trainer, so he became his friend Nobby's assistant at Harringay. Wal was eager to learn the tricks of the trade and they worked together on the ice hockey stars.

Nobby and Wal worked a lot on Joe Beaton, one of the very top ice hockey players. Joe had been the star of the Richmond Hawks until he received a serious groin injury in the 1936-37 season.

After speedway meetings at Belle Vue Manchester the fans and some of the riders would enjoy the attractions of the famous funfair. The riders liked to try their luck on the various stalls and would often win Teddy Bears. They knew that, apart from enjoying his garden, Nobby worshiped his blonde haired daughter, Doris, and from an early age her speedway Uncles would call on Nobby and leave the bears they had won at the fairground for her.

Because of his connection with the Canadian ice hockey players, when the Second World War started in 1939 Nobby was attached the Canadian Army at Purley. During those dark days leave was very infrequent and, when he did get time off, he had to take several trains to get home.

On one trip, an air raid, halted the train service from Waterloo. Nobby was going home and no German air raid going to stop him. So he set off on foot to get to his North London home. But he was injured in the raid and received kidney damage which was to cause his death some time later.

When Nobby did die, the family received letters of condolence from all round the world, proof of how much the sporting world thought of the world's best trainer.

My thanks to the late Keith Farman for his permission to use this article which originally appeared in The Speedway Researcher *in June 2007. Also, very special thanks to Nobby's daughter, Doris Newmark, for her assistance in the preparation of this article and for supplying the wonderful pictures.*

Above left: *Time off in an exotic location. It's a sunny afternoon sojourn for Wal Phillips, Nobby Key, Benny Kaufman and Nobby.*

Above right: *Lucky girl. Nobby's blonde haired daughter Doris, far left, shares a railway carriage – was it a trip back to London from Belle Vue – with one of America's best, Cordy Milne, her father and Geoff Pymar. Doris's rider 'Uncles' used to send her the Teddy Bears they won on the Belle Vue fairground stalls after the meetings.*

Friend to the ice stars. Cecilia Colledge, who was British, European and World Ice Dancing Champion sent an autographed picture to Nobby to thank him for helping her.

Chapter 30

THE NIGHT PRINCE PHILIP TURNED UP AT SPEEDWAY'S MEETING OF THE YEAR

MAYBE WE COULD PERSUADE THE PRINCE OF WALES'S SON TO COME TO CARDIFF FOR A GRAND PRIX

ALL THE gentlemen you see before you could, without being even the slightest bit fanciful, be described as speedway's *crème de la crème* . . . and without being too carried away by elevating them to 'speedway royalty', we'll just settle for the more modest speedway aristocrats.

In the near 90-year-old story of the sport in Britain there has probably never been such a golden seam of talent gathered in one place at one time. And never, in the field of speedway conflict, have so many turned up to cheer so few.

It is the Grand Parade before the Speedway Riders Championship Final at Wembley Stadium on Thursday, September 16th 1948. It would be another year before they got round to reinstating the World Championship, and the event at the time was the next best thing.

All speedway life was there – well, all speedway life that mattered, anyway. So let's identify them. From the right are: Vic Duggan (Harringay), Norman Parker (Wimbledon), Wilbur Lamoreaux (Wembley), Oliver Hart (Bradford), Ron Johnson (New Cross), Bill Longley (New Cross), Jack Parker (Belle Vue), Eric Chitty (West Ham) and, hidden, Bill Gilbert (Wembley). Behind them in the second row are, from the right, Ernie Price (Bradford), Jeff Lloyd (New Cross), Malcolm Craven (West Ham), Dent Oliver (Belle Vue), Lloyd Goffe (Harringay), Alec Statham (Wimbledon), Split Waterman (Wembley), Frank Hodgson (Middlesbrough), hidden Jack Biggs (Harringay).

What you cannot see in the darkness behind them is the 97,000 crowd that crammed into the Empire Stadium that night – more than watched the last Final at Wembley in 1981.

Actually there was real royalty on parade that night. Prince Philip Duke of Edinburgh. The riders were not only introduced to him before the racing, but he presented the prizes at the end of it all. It is the only known time that any one so close to the British monarch has ever attended a speedway meeting. It was the first, and it was the last. It has never – so far – happened again. Maybe someone can get on to his sporting grandson Prince William and suggest he goes along to a Grand Prix at Cardiff. After all, William's father is Prince of Wales.

Well, anyway, Australia's Vic Duggan was the winner. He received the trophy, and a cheque for the immense sum of £200 (they get something like that for a single point these days) from Prince Philip. Duggan's only point was dropped to England's Alec Statham who lost a run-off for second place with Australia's Ron Johnson.

Apparently the Duke was so 'spellbound' by his first speedway meeting that he 'refused an interval refresher'. According to my spy in the pits, the riders thought him 'a great guy'.

Chapter 31
TERRY, HOOKED AGAIN AND SITTING ON A FORTUNE

PORTAIT of a veteran who was bitten by the speedway bug . . . oh . . . when he was a lot younger than he is now, and he's still going strong. He says, and doesn't care who knows it: 'All my racing career was when speedway was fun. Those were The Good Old Days.'

You wouldn't be wrong if you sort of assumed that the gentleman in question has done a few laps round the speedway block: from Rye House, to Rayleigh and Exeter, Wolverhampton, New Cross, Hackney, Glasgow, Ipswich, to West Ham and Swindon.

He has a famous catchphrase: 'Keep the wheels turning and the plugs sparking.' And as he contemplates the approach of his 75th year in May he says he has no plans to stop doing either or hang up his leathers.

As you can see, he is not into kevlars, he still wears leathers, black ones, because he is a member of a collection of national speedway treasures – those magnificent Men In Black, whose mission in life is to show off those magnificent machines like the one in the picture, an original Dirt-Track Douglas. 'I always rode a JAP during my racing career, and still have two today' he says, 'but my 1928 Douglas is my favourite.'

The name is Terry Stone, one of whose other claims to fame is that he was the 2009 President of the World Speedway Riders Association.

He says: 'My Dad took me to West Ham just after the war. My favourite riders were Howdy Byford and Jack Young. And I raced cycle speedway for the Longbridge Leopards.

'I began riding speedway at Rayleigh in second halves. In those days the pay was £1 a start and £1 a point . . . BIG MONEY. Rayleigh closed and I was sold to Wolverhampton for £35 – a lot of money then. Later I was sold back to Rayleigh for £35 . . . at least I was consistent! I also rode for New Cross and then New Cross closed down – a bit of a pattern there.

'I was very lucky, having been at Rayleigh and Exeter, as both tracks were owned and managed by Pete Lansdale and Wally Mawdsley who certainly looked after me with rides.

'But no money was forthcoming from rider-promoter Trevor Redmond when I went to Glasgow. I lived with Joe Hicks and Bruce Ovenden, two New Zealanders, and I'm still in contact with Joe today.

'As well as riding I worked as a long distance lorry driver, often turning up to race in whichever lorry I was delivering. I stopped racing in 1973 as my wife Jean and I had three children to feed.

'Then I got involved with the Men In Black when I was asked to go to Hackney *(whose pre-war colours he is wearing)* where I was given an old bike to race on in the second half . . . hooked again.'

As well as being a member of the Men In Black demonstration team, Terry is a regular performer on grass tracks, at one of which this photograph was taken. And no wonder Terry's honorary spannermen are lavishing such TLC on that Douglas. How much is it worth? He said: 'The value is about £15,000 . . . if you can find one for sale.'

Well. You could say: stone me, Terry is sitting on a fortune.

Chapter 32
ADVANTAGE PARKER

OR A LESSON FROM MAESTRO JACK
ON HOW TO BAMBOOZLE THE OPPOSITION

FROM what appears to be going on here you might deduce that this somewhat preoccupied group has gathered round someone who is doing a passable impression of The Nutty Professor.

The Nutty Professor, you may recall was the title of a film about a grossly overweight character who took a special chemical that made him slim . . . but also obnoxious.

It's the glasses, of course, that makes the sharp suited gent sitting on the bike look more academic than speedway superstar. And the four characters hanging on his every word could also be called speedway superstars in their own right.

The name just discernable on the back mudguard of the bike is the real giveaway. It says Norman Parker.

The scene, as near as we can guess, is the pits at that magnificent old speedway emporium, Belle Vue Gardens at Hyde Road, Manchester.

Gathered in wrapt attention are, from left Norman Parker, then Wimbledon captain, and team mates Alec Statham, Jimmy Gibb, with Charles 'Pee Wee' Cullum on the right.

We can date the picture precisely – 1949 – and not only because of the vintage car in the background. We know the year because Canadian Jimmy Gibb, a pre-war star with West Ham, rode for Wimbledon for just the 1949 season. Incredibly Jimmy lived to celebrate his 102nd birthday, obviously believing in his own favourite catchphrase, which was: *Never Gibb Up*.

American Pee Wee Cullum, who had ridden before the war with the famous Putt Mossman stunt riders troup, rode for Belle Vue in 1949 and also in 1950, then went back home because the exchange rate between the pound and the dollar meant it was not financially worthwhile to ride for a British club any more.

Sound familiar?

The brilliant and super stylist Statham came within a single point of winning the world title substitute in 1948. He was the only rider to beat eventual winner Vic Duggan in the Speedway Riders Championship Final at Wembley, then lost a run-off with Ron Johnson for second place.

Finally to the 'Nutty Professor' himself, the incomparable Jack Parker, Norman's brother. Jack, arguably the most charismatic speedway rider England has yet produced in the sport's 89-year existence in Britain, had an unshakable belief in his own magnificent ability.

But he was never obnoxious as the Nutty Professor was: arrogant, yes, the supreme egotist, yes, but you could forgive him all of that because his unique ability was proven time and time again during his near three decades at the very top.

Now, what speedway knowledge do you think he might have been imparting to those eager onlookers? Well, if I know Mr Parker – and I think I came to over the years – he would be employing his mastery of his own highly intelligent brand of psychological gamesmanship.

The old maestro was probably telling Norman and his chums what was lacking on his brother's bike so that when his visiting Dons took to the track against Jack's Aces later on that day they would be in with no chance at all of victory. The maestro is setting about helping the home cause by bamboozling the opposition . . . if only just a little bit.

The declared Parker racing philosophy was: 'It does help if you have some kind of advantage.' As one devoted admirer once said: 'If Jack decided he was going to win he would win.'

Chapter 33
SUNNY JIM

SPEEDWAY'S TRAILBLAZER WITH THE ENIGMATIC MONA LISA SMILE

THE distance between an emotion-charged scene in a packed sporting arena, on one of the wilder nights of speedway triumph, to the tranquillity of tea in a quiet English country garden is precisely one lifetime.

In the first instance the night sky was rent by the roar of acclaim from 30,000 voices. The cheering was for one man clad in leathers, and what he had done ignited such enthusiasm that many eager hands lifted him up and bore him round the narrow ribbon of track beneath the arclights. He wore his prize, the proud symbol of conquest, a glittering, golden winged helmet. That was near 90 years ago.

The second instance, which took place very much closer to the present day, was altogether more proper. The number of people then could have been counted on one hand. The only sound was the low murmur of pleasant conversation and the tinkle of fine, delicate china.

But the gathering was for the same man, England's first speedway Test captain, Jim Kempster. 'Smiling' Jim.

Jim Kempster doesn't come blasting at you down the years like some of speedway's regular swashbucklers. It was the smile, of course. It was always there, as though there was always some secret part of him that he preferred not to reveal. Yes, there was definitely a touch of the Mona Lisa about Smiling Jim Kempster. It gave him something of an inscrutable and enigmatic look.

Some, just a few, of the secrets that made Jim Kempster what he was were told to me over that quiet country tea by Jim's sisters, Olive and Betty. They were living next door to each other in Poole, and I wouldn't have been surprised to learn that on Wednesday evenings, with the wind in the right direction, the sound of speedway motors carried into their back gardens from down in Wimbourne Road.

Their jim was one of the trailblazers of English speedway. One of the secrets Olive and Betty revealed to me was that Jim's name was not actually Jim. His proper name was Ernest Arthur David Kempster.

The stylish enigma. There is no mistaking why they called Jim Kempster Smiling Jim . . .

. . . And there is no mistaking the stylish way Jim went about trailbazing on the track.

Superstars of the Roaring Twenties. From left: Vic Huxley, Billy Lamont, Len Stewart, Jim, Ray Tauser and a very youthful ace mechanic Alec Moseley far right.

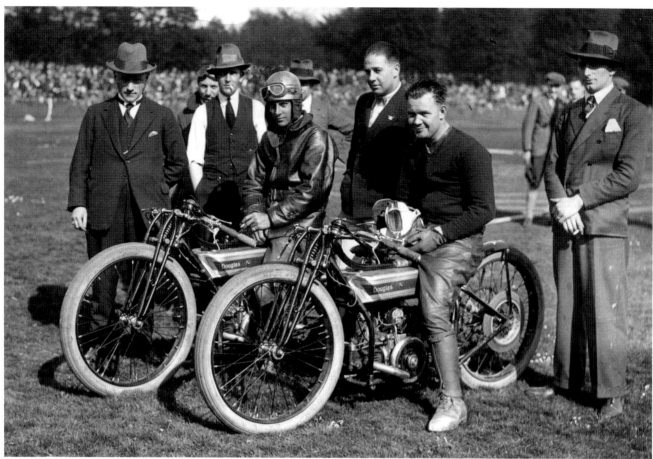

Help at hand. In the early days the crack Australians such as Vic Huxley (in the helmet) were obliging with advice but the American Cecil Broan (holding his helmet) taught Jim most of all. The picture was taken at High Beech.

He got the name Jim from the packet of breakfast cereal then popular in the young family's childhood.

According to Olive and Betty, the slogan 'Sunny Jim' was associated with the cereal and their brother always demanded his 'Sunny Jim' for breakfast every day.

The 'smiling' part came, said Olive, because Jim was always a joker. His pranks even got him banned from Sunday school. Everything he did was a game, and so that's why they called him Smiling Jim.

The family came from Leighton Buzzard in Bedfordshire. Young Jim got a job with Vauxhall Motors and began to take part in local motorcycling, grass track and speed events, often competing at the ultra fast Brooklands, the world's first purpose built motor racing circuit.

Olive said: 'Jim was often a passenger in sidecar races. He rode without boots so that he could almost fling himself out of the sidecar on the corners, clinging on just by his toes.'

When dirt track racing came to King's Oak, in the fateful and historic year of 1928, the only people who had mastered the technique of how to broadside high powered motorcycles were the invading Australian pioneers. Jim was there at the beginning to try out the new sport.

He was 27 and took to the newfangled national sensation so well that within three months he had landed a contract with International Speedways, the organisation masterminded by the Australian entrepreneur A. J. (Albert John) Hunting, whose company virtually controlled speedway throughout the country then.

Jim began to earn fame, and something of a fortune for the times. Now, of course he would have been considered well over the speedway hill to even contemplate making a living forging out a successful career on the track.

The Hunting empire had contracted most of the top stars of the day and Jim found himself in illustrious company. They included 'Wizard' Frank Arthur, 'Broadside' Vic Huxley, Billy 'The Cyclone' Lamont, Charlie Spinks and 'Flying' Dickie Smythe.

But Jim discovered that the Australians were always eager to help him and the American Cecil Brown taught Jim more than anyone.

Jim made his first appearance at the Wimbledon raceway on May 19, 1928 – and won £34 (more than £1,000 in today's money). A working man's weekly wage in those days was about £2.50 and to Jim the enormous amount of prize money was 'a Godsend'. He said: 'I went to that track with only the price of a half pint of Castrol in my pocket and by

the end of the evening I felt like a millionaire.'

In no time he had developed into a rider known for his flat-out, neck and neck attitude to racing with a grin that intimidated his opponents. Yet, off the track he was a quiet hero and a true sportsman.

His rapid rise soon began to earn him £100 (£3,000) a week. In handicap racing he was on an eight second start but because he did so well his start money was reduced and he soon found himself a scratch man along with the other major stars.

Then, as now, Jim found it was expensive to keep and maintain three or four machines in top racing condition. Yet, although the bikes were ostensibly the same in appearance, there was only one – the oldest – on which he could ride at his best and he never found out the reason.

Jim became the first Englishman to win a major trophy in competition with the best Australians when, on June 23 at White City, he won the Silver Sash, beating Huxley in his heat and Arthur, Smythe and Bishop in the final. The Silver Armlet *(such diverse and quaint trophies they had then)* followed on the same track and Jim's ambition then was to win the Golden Helmet, International Speedways' major trophy, at Wimbledon.

In his first attempt he lost to Frank Arthur in the final. It was several weeks later that he got the better of Huxley and Arthur to win the Golden Helmet at last. Which was the night 30,000 spectators 'went mad with delight' and carried him round the track shoulder high.

Jim's father saw it all, travelling all the way from Leighton Buzzard for the meeting because his son had told him that there was 'likely to be some exceptional racing'. Kempster Senior commented: 'As we see very little of him now that he is travelling between the White City in London, Wimbledon, Birmingham and Manchester I consented to go. I got the shock of my life. We are all very proud of him, and his brother Archie is now taking up the new sport.'

Contemporary newspaper reports detail the 'amazing and astonishing' crowd scenes

Above left: Star status. Jim displays his 'Star' number 14 before a Big Six match race series at Harringay in 1929 with Vic Huxley (centre) and Billy Dallison.

Above right: Skippering the 1930 Wimbledon side. Arthur Westwood is second from the left standing, Jim is next, then Len Stewart and Dicky Case with manager Dickie Maybrook right. In front Ernie Evans and Ray Tauser.

History makers. Local hero Jim leads the original England team which lost 30 – 17 to the Australians in the sensational first Test at Wimbledon in 1930. From the left: Jack Parker, Wal Phillips, Frank Varey, Jack Ormston, Roger Frogley and Jim. Reserve Gus Kuhn is unseen.

Triumph at Hyde Road. England's team that beat the Australians 51 – 45 in the fourth Test at Manchester in 1930 to wrap up the series. From left: Bob Harrison, Frank Charles, Jim, Squib Burton, Frank Varey, Walter Hull, Jack Parker and Eric Langton.

at the moment of Jim's triumph. His winning ride was, without doubt, the finest race of the year. 'Jim was behind for nearly three laps but, turning the wick up with good effect, won a very tight race in 82.6 seconds.'

Two weeks later the stadium was packed out again fort a special match race between Jim and Lloyd 'Sprouts' Elder. It was another triumph, Jim beating the American superstar in two straight runs.

In the brave, almost anything goes days that saw speedway establish itself as a major national sport, Jim Kempster literally rocketed to stardom. The Association Of Southern Dirt Track Promoters evolved a Star System by which the most prominent riders were given personal numbers: Sprouts Elder was No.4, Ron Johnson No.10, Vic Huxley No.11, Frank Arthur No.8. Among the Englishmen Colin Watson was No.16, Roger Frogley No.6 and Jim was No.14.

It was decided that no one should be awarded the No.1 because it would create jealousy among the star ranks. But somehow – and no one ever did find out exactly how – Tommy Croombs of West Ham managed to appropriate and ride as No.1.

In 1929, with the introduction of properly organised league racing, it was perhaps natural enough that Jim should become captain of Wimbledon, and the following year the leader of England at Wimbledon for the first historic Test match against the Australians on

Cartoon capers. The speedway press often delighted in depicting whimsical impressions of the big stars of the day.

'WIZARD' FRANK ARTHUR.   'SMILING' JIM KEMPSTER.

'BROADSIDE' VIC HUXLEY GETS A BIRD'S-EYE VIEW OF THE EXETER SPEEDWAY.

Above left: *Flying doubles. It's the brides' turn to smile as they pose for their double wedding day picture after their grooms, Roger Frogley, left, and Jim, had piloted themselves in for the ceremony.*

Above right: *The pioneers. Proud line-up of the first England touring team to visit New Zealand in 1930 - 31. From left: Norman Evans, George Greenwood, Roger Frogley, Squib Burton, Jim and Frank Bond.*

Left: *There's definitely a touch of the Mona Lisa here. Smiling Jim on the machine of the day at Belle Vue.*

*Speedy celebrities:
Jim with land and
water speed record
breaker Sir Malcolm
Campbell parade
sedately before the
Wimbledon crowd in
a jalopy that's hardly
the Campbell famous
car Bluebird.*

*Putting on the style
. . . and the
trademark smile: Jim
in portrait pose.*

30 June. To appoint the local hero captain of England was a shrewd Box Office enticement to the crowds.

At the advertised start time only strong men could force their way from one place to another within the jam-packed stadium. The first race had to be delayed three quarters of an hour, so huge were the queues to get in. It was an out and out sensation, and no matter that England lost 17 – 35. Jim skippered a team of all the English talents: Wal Phillips, Jack Parker, Frank Varey, Jack Ormston, Roger Frogley and Gus Kuhn . . . and he scored five points.

A slight mechanical blip, resulting in a temporary loss of form, was soon rectified with the help of mechanic Johnny Leete. Smiling Jim went on to win six trophy finals and shatter track records. He and Colin Watson dead heated in the Golden Helmet final at Harringay and Jim won the re-run. At Stamford Bridge's closing meeting Jim raised the match race record to 45.22 mph in beating Wal Phillips.

He was a member of the first English touring team to race in New Zealand in the 1930 – 31 close season in company with Norman Evans, George Greenwood, Roger Frogley, Squib Burton and Frank Bond. But before they set sail there was the little matter of a double wedding to take care of. Roger Frogley flew from his home at Hoddesdon and Jim flew from Stag Lane aerodrome on the same October day.

The shared honeymoon trip seemed to inspire the side which did well at Auckland, Wellington, Christchurch and Palmerston North. And they won a three match Test series.

Back in England the Frogleys, Roger and Buster, opened their flying school at Broxbourne and lots of riders became pilots. Smiling Jim was a regular, along with Wembley's George Greenwood, Jack Ormston and Harry Whitfield.

As with many of the early track stars, as the heady days of speedway's initial surge in popularity turned into something much more strictly formalised and regimented, Jim Kempster gradually ceased to be the force he was. He made a couple of attempts to ride himself back into the big time, one with Wembley, but they were not successful.

There had been stories of his fabulous earnings – £2700 (£81,000) in twelve weeks – and later he started a haulage business based in his native Leighton Buzzard.

Smiling Jim, having missed the First World War by a whisker, was determined to play what part he could in the second one. He closed down the haulage business and joined the Air Transport Auxillary (ATA) as a ferry pilot.

And then . . . tragedy: the plane Jim was delivering crashed. It was on 29 June, 1945, fifteen years almost to the day when Jim had captained that first historic England speedway Test team at Wimbledon, and Ironically one month after the war in Europe had come to an end.

His final fatal flight is recorded in a small booklet commemorating him and his ATA colleagues. The plane he was piloting struck communication wires over the River Rhine Gorge at Bingen. First Officer E.A.D Kempster's name is contained in the list of posthumous commendations at the back of the ATA booklet. Its title: Brief Glory.

Chapter 34
ON HIS MAJESTY'S SERVICE: HEROES WITH A MISSION

THESE two likely lads are severely intent on doing serious damage to the nefarious ambitions of that evil little man who was described by *Dad's Army* Commanding Officer Captain Mainwaring as 'looking like Charlie Chaplin'.

What's more, they succeeded.

On the left is Jack Gordon of the Royal Navy and on the right is George Pepper of the Royal Air Force. Both of them could have come fresh off the parade ground with their boots blacked and their immaculate uniforms.

It is 72 years since they could claim Mission Accomplished next to their names. The sad part of it is that only one of them was able to celebrate it.

They are posed in the pits at Jack's parent club Belle Vue where, as we all know, the speedway flag was kept flying throughout the entire duration of the conflict. The bike is hardly a machine they were used to, but maybe that and their weekend passes got them there. Were they there to race in one of the wartime meetings? We don't know because they are not in leathers.

Bolton born Jack began his love affair with speedway racing at Liverpool in 1934 at the age of 19. A brief spell at Edinburgh revealed his potential in 1936 when he became the local Match Race Champion.

When war did come as a naval officer he took part in three landings in the Mediterranean and Europe. He was allocated to Northern League championship winning Middlesbrough in 1946 to cover for injured captain Frank Hodgson, and the following year he posted a star-rating ten point average with the Bears – but rode in only two matches for them.

Destined for higher things, George Pepper leads the 1939 Newcastle team. The riders are, from the left, Bill Goodall, Fred 'Kid' Curtis, Syd Littlewood, Reg Hay, George, on bike, Billy Lamont, Johnnie Hoskins, Bonnie Waddell, Norman Hargreaves. Kneeling Rol Stobart.

PHOTO GORER   NEWCASTLE ON TYNE

NEWCASTLE SPEEDWAY TEAM 1939

Man of many parts. Jack Gordon aboard his speedway machine, but he was also an expert horseman, tennis player and boxer . . . as well as a war hero.

Later that year he captained Wigan Warriors, but in 1948 he had a disastrous season at Bristol, which he once listed as his favourite track, where he dislocated a shoulder in a crash and scored precisely nothing. The next years found him at Coventry and then Sheffield, but his form gradually deteriorated and he retired in 1950.

Apart from speedway Jack was an expert horseman, tennis player and boxer.

George Pepper was a Canadian destined to be in the same class as West Ham's top liners Eric Chitty and Jimmy Gibb. Before coming to Britain he was a road racer, winning the Canadian 200 mile street race in 1936.

He arrived in Britain in 1938 intending to ride in the Isle of Man TT Races, but Chitty and Gibb persuaded George to try speedway racing. At First Division West Ham promoter Johnnie Hoskins sent him to his Second Division track at Newcastle.

George was an immediate star at Newcastle and set a three lap track record which stood well into the post-war seasons. Many experts predicted he was destined for the sport's highest honours. But for the war it is certain he would have joined Chitty and Gibb at West Ham for the 1940 season.

Jeff Lloyd, post-war star at Newcastle, New Cross and Harringay, recalled the hard Pepper racing style when riding for Bristol in 1939. Pepper deprived him of a maximum and Lloyd said of George's tactics: 'Considering my inexperience, he was far more aggressive than he need have been in beating me.' Both wanted to be the best and rode to achieve that.

After becoming a pilot with the RAF's 29 Squadron, George was as distinguished in combat as he was on the speedway track, shooting down six enemy aircraft and being awarded the Distinguished Flying Cross and Bar. He and his co-pilot were known as Salt & Pepper.

George died aged 26 in a flying accident in a Mosquito on 17 November, 1942. He is buried in his home town of Belleville, Ontario, Canada.

CANNY WILF, THE MAN WHO SAVED BELLE VUE

HAD it not been for this man speedway may not have succeeded in defying Hitler. Maybe that is stretching things just a little bit, but had he not been able to help out Belle Vue, who kept the sport going every weekend with the 'We Never Closed' wartime meetings, they might have . . . well, closed.

The gent being so closely observed concentrating on warming up his bike is one of speedway's largely unsung heroes, Wilf Plant. After graduating from the Midlands pre-war grass tracks, he struggled to get rides at Leicester, West Ham, New Cross, Wimbledon and Leeds. Then, just as he thought he'd cracked it with Middlesbrough in 1939, the war came and he spent the duration doing his bit repairing tractors at his Melton Mowbray garage.

Which is how he came to save the day at Hyde Road. Belle Vue manager Alice Hart and West Ham's Eric Chitty, on a return trip from London, broke down outside the Plant emporium. It turned out they had been to try and get a supply of fuel for the Saturday afternoon meetings.

Canny Wilf just happened to have a supply of cut-price fuel. His was three shilling a gallon (15p) compared with the more usual price of 7s.6d (37p). Wilf said: 'I did a deal with Miss Hart who booked me in every meeting. I took the fuel and I also made and repaired spare parts, which kept the bikes going.

'We used to get paid for riding. Not points money. For instance Jack Parker got £40 and I got a tenner. Jack seemed to get paid for doing nowt. But he had the name of course, he was a brilliant rider.'

Those wartime outings mixing with such big stars as Parker in Manchester must have done Wilf good, because when league racing resumed in 1946 he was part of the fabulously successful Middlesbrough side which won back-to-back Northern League (Division 2) titles in the first two seasons after the war. Only two riders outscored Wilf in 1946, the brilliant Bert Spencer of Norwich, and Sheffield's Stan Williams. He was even better than Newcastle's Jeff Lloyd who swiftly went to First Division New Cross.

Between times, Wilf and Eric Chitty organised the unique Entertainments National Service Association (ENSA) team of top stars that toured occupied Europe in the winters of 1945 and 1946 entertaining the troops. Two of them are his fascinated watchers in the picture.

Naturally Wilf began to attract the attention of other top clubs, but a bid by Bristol who bulldozed to the title in 1948 was turned down. Instead he stayed at Cleveland Park until, with the club becoming the victim of its own success and failing to complete its fixtures, Wilf went to Fleetwood for a Divison 2 record £1,000 transfer fee.

There were brief spells at Coventry and Long Eaton before he hung up his leathers in 1952 at the – for those days – comparatively early age of 36.

Wilf's son Graham followed his father onto the speedways, winning the Second Division Riders Championship in 1968 while, appropriately, with Middlesbrough.

Chapter 35
STAR-SPANGLED SEND OFF BY THE WIZARD OF DRIBBLE

THERE are one or two familiar faces in this line-up. If we are honest, to describe them as distinguished does scant justice to at least two of the personalities on view.

Speedway fans will recognize instantly . . . or ought to . . . the two riders whose bike is arousing so much interest among the obviously fascinated group around them. Our pair of intrepid track stars are, in the centre, Jack Gordon, the first captain of Fleetwood, and next to him team mate Frank Malouf.

The occasion is the opening of the Fleetwood track in 1948, and the curious onlookers are members of the Blackpool football team who have been dragooned into giving the speedway boys a star-spangled send-off. From the left are Alex Munro, Eric Hayward, Eddie Shimwell and those two celebrated England internationals Sir Stanley Matthews – the Wizard Of Dribble himself, no less – and, trying the bike out for size, Stan Mortensen. The gentleman in the flat 'at, on the right, is not named.

Riders who wore the distinctive Fleetwood race jacket, a red star on a green background, were popular Division 2 visitors in the first few post-war seasons, and included, Dick Geary, Norman Hargreaves, Wilf Plant, Cyril Cooper, Reg Lambourne, Jack Winstanley and the up-and-coming Dick Seers.

Fleetwood had replaced Wigan Warriors who had closed after only one season, but the Flyers were not a combination that really took off. They were always in the basement region of the league and the club came to a dramatic end in 1952. Its two promoters were jailed for defrauding local businessmen out of £20,000 in their efforts to set up another speedway in Blackpool.

They were Joseph Waxman, 53, of Blackpool, who was jailed for two-and-a-half years, and James Wolfenden, 49, from Stockport, who was jailed for two years. They ran into trouble because, it was said, there were 'insufficient funds available for their existing speedway club at Fleetwood'.

Despite such a sad and ignominious demise, during its brief period of operation, from the opening in 1948 to the closure 1952, when a few open meetings were staged, Fleetwood speedway captured the imagination of the locals and today many people retain happy memories of the track and the team.

One grandmother, who did not wish to be named, remembered attending matches with her husband on Wednesday nights and said: 'It was very exciting because you had four fellows racing around the track on these motorbikes and anything could happen.'

Well, yes, madam. It certainly did to those two over-ambitious fraudsters, Waxman and Wolfenden. They were never to return to the town, and to this day no one is sure what became of them.

Chapter 36
OUTRAGE !

DIRT-TRACKER APPEARS IN POSH ROTTEN ROW

WHEN speedway was very, very young, it attracted the imagination of not only the entire nation, but also that of H.M (Henry Mayo) Bateman, one of the most brilliant and funniest cartoonists of the day.

His work depicted comically exaggerated reactions to minor and usually upper-class social gaffes, such as *The Man Who Lit His Cigar Before the Royal Toast, The Dandelion That Appeared On The Centre Court At Wimbledon* and . . . *The Dirt-Track Rider Who Appeared In Rotten Row.*

Speedway, known as dirt-track racing in the Roaring Twenties, was the new wonder of the sporting world. It was the Jazz Age, when all kinds of crazy things suddenly burst upon a good-time hungry youth . . . mass motoring, talking pictures and global exploration that came with the discovery of heavier-than-air flight.

As the Bright Young Things of the day charlestoned the nights away, nothing seemed more dangerously attractive, or as thrilling, as being part of a massed crowd witnessing daring young men hurling high-powered motorcycles round small, enclosed dirt tracks.

Which is why H. M. Bateman used a dirt-track rider to lampoon the posh pastime of the elitists who liked to demonstrate their elevated social standing by taking a morning ride in that famous bridleway, Rotten Row, in Hyde Park – and still do to this day.

THE DIRT-TRACK RIDER WHO APPEARED IN ROTTEN ROW

Bateman's cartoons caused a sensation. He drew for top magazines such as *Punch* and *Tatler*, and by the 1930s he was being acclaimed as a genius. He was also earning a personal fortune – more than £5,000 a year, or £155,000 in today's money.

Fittingly, as Australia was the birthplace of speedway racing as we now know it, Bateman was born in Australia. Thwarted of his ambition to become a serious painter, he went on to perfect his unique cartoon style which was inspired by comic book characters.

This dirt-track one is typical – showing the subject, with all the attention focused on him, blithely carrying on, innocent of the outrage he has caused. Bateman singled out for scrutiny not only the individual committing the 'offence' but, perhaps more interestingly, the society that condemned him.

During World War Two Bateman illustrated posters for the government – one of which was a famous catchphrase of the time: *Coughs And Sneezes Spread Diseases, Help To Keep Your Nation Fighting Fit, Trap The Germs In Your Handkerchief.*

In later life there was an increasingly acrimonious battle with the Inland Revenue, and he died in 1970, his 84th year, on Gozo where he had lived simply and modestly.

An English Heritage blue plaque, unveiled in 1997, commemorates Bateman at 40 Nightingale Lane in Clapham where he lived between 1910 and 1914.

Chapter 37
THE NIGHT ERNIE'S LUCK RAN OUT

NOT since the great pre-war days of Jack and Cordy Milne and Wilbur Lamoreaux had there been such a shining talent with the ability to put the Stars And Stripes back on top of the speedway world.

Charles 'Pee-Wee' Cullum had spent a couple of years with Belle Vue. He was a steady scorer, but had not really elevated himself into what you might call world class. Then, along came Ernie Roccio, a pleasant, extremely handsome young man you couldn't help liking. His personality was different. And all too briefly he graced the sport with Wimbledon between 1950 and 1952.

That's him in the action picture at Wembley, on the outside of Lions Trevor Redmond and Tommy Price with his partner Ronnie Moore at the back.

To begin with there was a tug of war for his signature between Wimbledon and Birmingham. His first attempt to sign for Birmingham ended when he ran into labour permit problems and was promptly sent back to Los Angeles. Eventually Wimbledon got their man and Ernie made his debut for the Dons in June 1950.

Within weeks he was on double figure scores, and the following year Ernie qualified for the World Final. But on 22 July 1952 he broke down on the way to ride at West Ham and is quoted as saying: 'This will not be my lucky night.' It turned out to be the night his luck ran out.

The meeting went to a last heat decider. The track was wet, and down to ride for West Ham were Wal Morton and Kid Curtis and for Wimbledon Cyril Maidment and Barry Briggs. West Ham needed a 5 - 1 to force a draw. Wimbledon boss Ronnie Greene replaced the young and inexperienced Barry Briggs with Ernie to try and save the match.

According to promoter Johnnie Hoskins's later programe notes: 'There was jubilation in the Wimbledon camp and there was little hope in ours . . . but suddenly the Hammers were leading. Then, on the third bend with the Hammers well in front, there was a crash . . . the Wimbledon riders had collided.'

An eyewitness in the crowd recalled: 'Ernie tried all he new to split the Hammers pair. He was unable to see through his eye shield, which he discarded and was struck in the eye by flying wet shale. Ernie's front wheel touched Cyril's back wheel and, unable to see, he lost control of his machine, careering into the fence at speed and then went into a lamp post.' West Ham had won with that last heat 5 – 0. And Ernie died from his injuries a few hours later.'

The flamboyant West Ham chief, Johnnie Hoskins, couldn't resist a typically emotional tribute to Ernie in his following week's match programme. He wrote: 'The fatal accident to Ernie has upset everyone in the speedway game, particularly the riders. Still, the show goes on. There never was a worthwhile sport in which no accident occurred . . . and it will continue to go on while there are men to ride the machines. Speedway racing is a rough, tough, strenuous game . . . it is full of disappointment, joy and hope. The path to glory is ever upwards and on the way, sometimes, someone pays the supreme sacrifice.'

At Wimbledon's next meeting, the Dons and visiting Belle Vue riders lined up to silently honour the fallen hero, his machine elevated in lonely tribute, with Ronnie Greene (extreme right) standing straight in respect. At home, Ernie's mother pleaded with her other speedway rider son, Johnnie, to give up the game. And he never rode again.

It was to be a full quarter of a century before another American, Scott Autrey, reached anywhere near the Roccio class.

Swift success. Ernie Roccio in Wimbledon's colours . . . his fatal accident upset everyone in the speedway game .

Chapter 38
THE MITTAGONG FLASH

THEY called him the Mittagong Flash. His real name is Keith Ryan from New South Wales. But in rough, tough Glasgow the local Tigers speedway fans knew him as Buck Ryan. His promoter, Johnnie S Hoskins, always alert to the best publicity angle, named him 'Buck' Ryan after the popular cartoon superhero in the *Daiiy Mirror* newspaper.

Keith was born in the beautiful Southern Highlands at Mittagong, New South Wales, on 30 December 1922, the second son of a schoolteacher. He was never able to play truant from school because his father taught at the same school.

His interest in all things motorcycle came early. At the age of 16 he had saved seven pounds, enough to buy a 1928 BSA. Later he owned fifteen different road bikes, including a Rudge, AJS, Manx Norton and an Excelsior He joined the Waverley and District Motorcycle Club with close friend Vic Duggan in 1939 and competed in road race events. The same year Keith was second in the NSW 250cc state Championship on an AJS.

Keith was appriticed to the De Havilland Aircraft Company at Alexandria. After completing a course in tool making he was promoted to shop foreman. The interest in speedway followed a visit to Sydney Showground in 1938 where he was thrilled by the riding of Max Grosskreutz, Billy Lamont and Wally Little.

His first speedway bike was bought from old time rider Noel Thompson, and he practised on the local mudflats with Vic and Ray Duggan, Graham Warren and Frank Dolan. Any further speedway plans were halted by the war, and the bike was sold to Bernard 'Bat' Byrnes from Burwood. The pair would later ride for the same team in Scotland.

After an attempt to enlist in the RAAF it was decided that his talents were needed in the aircraft industry with De Havilands and he worked alongside the Duggans and English rider Cliff Parkinson on the development of the Mosquito fighter bomber.

At the end of the war Keith's speedway career took off at the Sydney Sports Ground. In late 1945 he was spotted by promoter Frank Arthur who was on the look out for riders for his new venture at Brisbane Exhibition Ground. The team of Sydney riders who appeared at the Brisbane track for the Night Speed Carnival on 20 April 1946 included Keith, Archie Neil, Hugh Geddes, Keith Gurtner and Harold Gillett. They were later joined by Victorians Ron 'Junior' Bainbridge Andy Menzies, Owen Gyles and Morrie Bond.

It was at the Exhibition track on 21 December, the final meeting prior to his return to Sydney for the Christmas break. that Keith suffered a serious neck injury which, it seemed would halt his career.

The accident happened in the Vic Huxley handicap final when the front runners, Bruce Campbell. Norm Burke and Cyril Romaine fell. Keith, who was on a 130 handicap, ran over a machine to avoid a fallen rider. His bike somersaulted and landed on his chest. He received fractures to his upper chest and neck that sidelined him for four months.

Although unable to ride for the remainder of the Australian season, veteran Queenslander Charlie Spinks recommended Keith should race in England. An arrangement was set up with legendary promoter Johnnie S. Hoskins for a trial for the Glasgow White City Tigers. As Keith considered Hoskins to be a father figure it was with confidence that he embarked on the voyage into the unknown in March 1947. Already signed for the Tigers were Ron 'Junior' Bainbridge, Cecil 'Gruff' Garland and Bat Byrnes. The fact that the Glasgow team had four Australians would cause problems for Keith in a later season.

Keith paid his own fare to England, travelling to Southampton on 22 March, 1947 aboard the former troopship the Asturius. Fellow passengers were: Junior Bainbridge and

Spotted . . . by Frank Arthur. Keith at Brisbane's Exhibition Ground, but a crash that threatened his career was to come.

Where Johnnie Hoskins got the name Buck Ryan from. An illustration of the contemporary newspaper cartoon character Buck Ryan risking all by riding a motorcycle without a helmet.

Made it to England and the Glasgow side. Now named 'Buck' by Johnnie Hokins, Keith's team mates were, from the left: Nobby Downham, Harold Fairhurst, Will Lowther, Norman Lindsay, Ian Hoskins. Kneeling: Keith (with hidden neck brace), Gordon McGregor, Junior Bainbridge and Bat Byrnes.

Bat Brynes who were both headed for Glasgow. There was also Arthur Payne, Jack Kidd, Bill Harris, Reg Challenger, going to Tamworth, Jack Baxter to Wigan, Bonnie Waddell to Newcastle, Ken LeBreton New Cross and Mal Hodgson Bradford.

First stop in England was to Harringay speedway, which was a home from home for Australian riders. Already on the Racers books were Keith's Sydney friends Vic and Ray Duggan and Frank Dolan. Also in the team were Buck Whitby, Jackie Biggs and Jack Arnfield. According to London journalist John Hyam, Keith, Norman Lindsay and Bat Byrnes were actually signed up for Harringay but Keith and Norman were exchanged with a cash adjustment for Wal Morton who rode for Glasgow Tigers in 1946.

On a bleak day in March Keith arrived in Scotland to meet Johnnie Hoskins who had put his son Ian in charge of the Second Division Glasgow team. Lindsay and Byrnes rode a few matches for Harringay before joining Keith at Glasgow.

Keith disguised the fact that he had received a serious neck injury in case it would prohibit his chances of getting a team place. He wore a neck brace unknown to his promoter, quite a risk to take but it paid off.

When Johnnie Hoskins decided Keith would be billed as Buck after the comic strip character, the name stuck and for the remainder of his British career at least he became Buck Ryan.

The first meeting for Keith was Wednesday 30 April 1947 against Wigan Warriors. Team mates that night were captain Joe Crowther, Will Lowther, Bill Baird, Bert Shearer, Junior Bainbridge and Angus McGuire. The team had already ridden four matches and Keith, In his first ride, followed partner Bill Baird home to ensure a drawn heat. His third place was a paid abonus point. The system was that if you finished behind your partner in either second or third spot you were paid a bonus point for the same score as him. The pay at that time was £1 a point. Keith became a good team man scoring many bonus points in his 89 matches for the Tigers over three seasons.

Team riding was an art that Keith was to learn. Wily veteran Joe Crowther was a master of the art only too happy to pass on his experience to the young Aussie. In his second meeting Keith got his first heat win, shepherded home by Joe, which was followed up in his second ride when he teamed up with Bill Baird to score another maximum heat win. The Tigers fans were ecstatic.

After another home meeting Keith had to face the reality of the tremendous travel involved in British speedway when the Tigers embarked on a southern tour. Meetings at Bristol, Norwich and Middlesborough, followed by a return to Glasgow, made it clear to Keith that driving miles and miles on winding roads, often in rain and stopping at roadside cafes were the least glamorous side of a speedway rider's life.

Team events are the bread and butter for the professional speedway rider, a booking for

Master of the art of team riding, veteran Joe Crowther. Under the Crowther tuition Keith matured and they became a formidable pairing.

Above left: *Buck's favourite partner – as well as Joe Crowther – Bat Byrnes, a fine all round motorcyclist and mechanic.*

Above right: *The bruiser. Alec 'Farmer' Grant who 'unseated Buck in a robust clash at Ashfield. At the time, Alec was the only one-eyed speedway rider.*

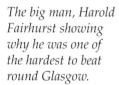

The big man, Harold Fairhurst showing why he was one of the hardest to beat round Glasgow.

an open meeting is the jam. The disadvantage for a Northern based rider is that outside bookings are few and far between. Keith gained one of those rare opportunties with a ride for a Northern team against Harringay at Norwich on 10 May. He showed a liking for the large Norwich track and scored 5 points.

Teaming up for a Best Pairs meeting with Joe Crowther in July they ran third in very good company. Another milestone was a spot in the Overseas team against England at Glasgow. Keith contributed a handy six points, but the English team won 66-52.

Missing three meetings in August due to injury Keith was back in the team for his best score of the season with 7 plus two bonus points in the home match with Norwich.

Another valuable booking came with a place in the Overseas team against England at Glasgow on August 8th, his six points were not enough to stop the home side winning 68-42.

The final meeting of 1947 in Britain for Keith was at Wigan on 20 September. Then it was back to the docks to board ship for the long voyage home. In his first season he had ridden in 30 official meetings scoring a total of 68 points with an average of 4.2. He had also ridden small tracks like Bristol, and bigger circuits of Norwich and Wigan, not bad experiences for a new boy.

Ian Hoskins in his excellent book *The Speedway Hoskins* tells how Keith and Junior matured as riders from green beginners. Ian also tells the tales of Ryan, the fun-loving

character, who had many off track escapades. One was after hitting a gatepost and demolishing the headlight of his car, he reversed and did the other. The theory being it was no good with one so might as well knock the other one out

After a winter in the Australian sunshine with a less hectic programme Keith was fit and eager for his second season for Glasgow in 1948. During the Australian season he had carefully chosen his meetings, riding mainly at the Sydney Showground where he was on a 90 yard handicap.

Accompanied by his wife Mavis he arrived in Glasgow in time for the opening match on Wednesday March 31st against Newcastle.

Keith's 7 points in the opening match were a clear message he meant business in 1948. The league had expanded with the addition of Edinburgh, which would prove good for local derbies and less travelling. The second meeting against Wigan confirmed he was going to be a force to be reckoned with, cruising to equal his highest score of paid 9. The purple patch had begun, a paid 11 against Birmingham. On 8 May Keith was at Norwich in an Australian side against Second Division stars in which he scored 4 points.

Four days later the headline in the *Speedway Reporter* magazine blazed: *Record Crowd See Glasgow Win*. It was an account of the home meeting between Tigers and visiting Edinburgh. The match report said: 'Over 20,000 fans – the best crowd of the season – turned out for the all-Scottish clash between Glasgow and Edinburgh at the White City . . . . after some of the best racing seen at the circuit, the local Tigers triumphed by 49 points to 35.

'Joe Crowther returned to something like his best form and with Buck Ryan (both) scored (12-point) maximums for Glasgow. Recently promoted to heat leader this was Ryan's first maximum since he came to this country nearly two years ago.'

Speedway News described the atmosphere as 'just like pre-war days again . . . this Northern League match proved just as thrilling as those of former days. Crowther and Ryan got going for the home lot (and) put paid to Edinburgh's hopes of victory'.

Another open meeting came up on 15 May, the Caledonian cup at Edinburgh. He must have pleased the Monarch's promotion because he was invited back for the 50 Guinea Trophy on 12 June.

In July a Glasgow Select which was in essence the regular Tigers with Middlesbrough's Frank Hodgson, faced a team with a couple of Tigers, Graham Warren and Edinburgh men Clem Mitchell, Dick Campbell and Eddie Lack who were led by the great Vic Duggan. Vic agreed to take part, not for the promise of appearance money, but for the chance of playing his beloved golf on the famed course at St Andrews.

After the golf Vic had a good night at White City. He was defeated by only Frank Hodgson in the match after a close run race, and by Graham Warren in the second half qualifier. In the final he tangled with Crowther and wrecked his bike. A sporting Keith loaned Vic his bike and the star Aussie used it to win the rerun.

June 16th saw the National Trophy match with arch rivals Edinburgh and his highest score of 13 paid 15. The high scores continued throughout the season.

The home match with Bristol in July was one that Keith would want to forget. After a single point in his first ride he suffered an ankle injury in Heat 7 and retired from the meeting. The Tigers were still able to score a convincing win over the Bulldogs.

A painful memory of the 1948 season was a close encounter with Sheffield's Bruce Semmens, a rider known to take no prisoners. Semmens introduced Keith to the Owlerton safety fence after a torrid four laps causing mutiple fractures to his right foot and a four week lay off. The incident made Keith realise there were riders to be wary of.

Selected for the British Riders Championship rounds at Fleetwood and Edinburgh Keith scored 4 points and 1 point. During the season he rode 24 official league matches scoring a total of 149 points giving an average of 6.21. This placed him fourth in the Tigers' score chart and should have guaranteed his team place for 1949. This was to become an issue the following season.

The final match for Glagow Tigers in 1948 was held at Edinburgh, on 18 September. It

Study in contemplation: Buck takes time to think . . . and polish his goggles.

Above left: Out front for Glasgow. Buck leads team mate Nobby Downham with Gruff Garland and Norman Evans in their wake.

Above right: Back home. Buck in a close confrontation with Ken LeBreton (in only half his trademark white leathers) at Sydney.

was a challenge match against Sheffield as the home team was away. Then it was again time for the voyage home to prepare for the Australian season.

Keith recalled that 1948 season in an interview with noted Australian journalist Steve Magro in 1998:

'Our captain Joe Crowther and New Zealander Harold Fairhurst were the hardest to beat around Glasgow. It was a good track when you got the hang of it. You would go for it on the long straights, but the flat bends were very sharp.

'My favourite tracks were Bradford and Norwich. I didn't like the small Middlesbrough track, it also rained every time I went there.

'My favourite partner was Bat Byrnes who was an all round motorcyclist, he had won the Australian TT at Bathurst in 1939, 1940 and again in 1949. He was also a fine mechanic, but his career ended after a bad accident at Norwich.'

Back in Sydney for the 1948-49 season there was a change in the traditional format of Australian speedway with the introduction of nine heat team racing. This new presentation was not universally popular as it caused a reduction in the number of speedcar and sidecar events.

Solo Teams were formed at Sydney Showground, Sydney Sports Ground and Newcastle. Keith joined the Newcastle side, which was drawn from visiting Wimbledon rider Norman Parker, Bill Rogers, Aub Lawson, Don Lawson, Cliff Watson Bill Melluish Arthur Payne and Mick Callaghan. It was no surprise that Newcastle with three English First division riders in the team won the league.

International recognition at last. Wearing the Australian race jacket for the first time in the fifth Test against England at Sydney in 1951 Keith takes his place in a star-studded line-up of, from the left, Lionel Van Praag, Dick Seers, Aub Lawson, manager, Jack Arnfield, Keith. Kneeling, Lionel Levy, Ken LeBreton and Jack Gates.

Keith returned to Scotland in 1949 for the third time ready to put on the red and white Tigers colours for the 13 April meeting. The Second Division had expanded with the addition of Coventry, Cradley Heath, Ashfield, Southampton and Walthamstow. This gave Keith five new tracks to ride. The inclusion of Ashfield Giants only a few miles from the Tigers at Ibrox Park gave some extra local rivalry. The Giants, also promoted by Johnnie Hoskins, had five Australians in the team Gruff Garland, Merv Harding, Keith Gurtner, Ken LeBreton and Jack Martin. The Ashfield team introduced coloured leathers for the first time in speedway history with Harding in red, Gurtner in blue and Ken LeBreton in his famous white.

The Speedway Riders Association [SRA], the riders' union, was fearful of reduced opportunities for British riders because of the increased influx from overseas. Many southern based English riders objected to riding in the north, so the SRA's rule of three overseas riders per team was relaxed for northern clubs. But in 1949 the SRA took a harder line, which was to have repercussions for Keith.

Australia made a brief excursion into team racing, and Keith was one of the top talent in this Newcastle side. Back row from the left: Aub Lawson, Keith, Junior Bainbridge, Bill Rogers, Oliver Hart. Front: Gruff Garland and Ron Clarke.

With a new machine he was ready for a good season. Two meetings had been missed but eventually he took to the track against new boys Coventry, starting off with a score of 7. The first away meeting at Southampton he was heading for a maximum with three wins only to fall in his fourth ride.

An early meeting at Ashfield reported in *Speedway Gazette* mentioned an encounter with the robust north countryman Alec 'Farmer' Grant:

'Earlier in the meeting LeBreton had been excluded for dumping Will Lowther from his machine after the Tiger had beaten him from the traps. Giants' Alex Grant went out of Heat 14 for unseating Ryan, a race that ultimately had only one finisher due to a fall, an engine failure and an exclusion. Tigers, who stuck to the white line, had it wrapped up before the last race.'

An open meeting at Ashfield on 3 May saw Keith in the familiar Kangaroo body colours for a scratch team labelled the Kangaroos against Ashfield. He had a good night scoring 5 paid 6.

On the visit to Cradley Heath on 6 May he sustained injuries that would keep him out of the team for a few weeks. This incident was reported in *Speedway Gazette*:

'Tigers were a poor side, described as docile, failing to challenge the home men in most races at the once hard-to-find Midlands venue of Dudley Wood Stadium at Cradley Heath . . . Buck Ryan broke his toes when he fell in Heat 14 and this injury would rule him out of action for a few weeks. This ended a poor night for the Aussie who scored one paid two.'

He was fit by 16 June but then the blow fell. He was banned. Fellow Sydney rider Bat Brynes, a late arrival due to competing in the Australian TT, took Keith's place when the SRA enforced the three Australians per team ruling.

It was a hard time for Keith. Although he rode for two weeks in the Glasgow second half and in the World Championship round at Newcastle on 6 July scoring 3 points, a professional rider needs to be racing continually. The matter was resolved on 9 July for the match at Coventry. Making up for lost time he was in a determined mood for the home match with Ashfield reeling off three straight wins until halted by an uncharacteristic engine failure. Keith's machines were always of a high standard. During his time with the Tigers only three engine failures were recorded.

At the end of August Keith was in a team labelled Scotland that met a Dutch team at the Olympic Stadium in Amsterdam. It was a strange looking 'Scottish' team, tracking three Australians. However they beat the locals 38-34. The following day they travelled to Feyenoord. This time riding as Glasgow Tigers and losing 39-45.

The end of the season was coming, also the end of Keith's British career. His last meeting in Britain was against Fleetwood on 5 October going out with a 7 paid 10 total. In that last season he had ridden 33 official league matches with an average of 5.07 from a score of 130 plus 26 bonus points. Clearly the upset from the ban did not help him in his final season.

One character that Keith became involved with at Glasgow was the infamous Joe 'The Whaler' Ferguson. Joe went to sea in a whaling ship in the Antartic to raise the funds for a speedway bike. He later bought one from Keith who instructed him in the rudiments of racing then let him loose on the Tigers' track. Joe fell off at every bend, persisting for two

Challenging 'England's best, Jack Parker on the inside, Keith could match anyone on Australian tracks. Others being treated to a view of his back wheel are Tommy Miller (left) and Ron Clarke.

hours. Eventually the big crash came and Keith helped remove the remains of a once pristine Ryan speedway bike from the track. Joe became a folk legend in Scotland as he came back time after time, but never made the grade, although it was worth the entry fee just to see him try.

Keith began his 1949-50 Australian season in Brisbane on 19 November. The long awaited call came for the Australian Test team on February 3 for the fifth Test against England at the Sports Ground and it was there that Keith proudly wore the famous white kangaroo on the red race jacket for the first time.

In Heat 8 he combined with Aub Lawson for a 5-1 over Jack Parker, an outstanding ride to beat Parker, the English captain, who had finished second in the 1949 World Final at Wembley.

Apart from Parker, there were some very good riders in the England team but they were beset by machinery problems and lack of workshop facilities. Fred Williams, Dent Oliver and Oliver Hart were all class performers but failed to produce their true form that summer. Williams went on to be a double World Champion,

Keith also won a Best Pairs meeting at the Showground paired with the visiting American Wilbur Lamoreaux. They defeated 1937 World Champion Jack Milne, his brother Cordy and a host of top Australian and English riders that night.

Keith's season ended early as a result of laying down to avoid a fallen Bill Melluish only to be hit by Gruff Garland's machine. The crankcase of Gruff's machine hit Keith's right arm and shoulder causing a break which was to trouble him for the rest of his life.

Despite overtures from the Glasgow promoters for the 1950 season in Scotland he resisted and elected to stay in Australia and prove his status as one of Australia's best riders in the Tests against England.

For the Brisbane and Adelaide Tests the riders were flown to the meeting by Lionel Van Praag and many said they were on a wing and a prayer on that trip. The total tally for Keith of 76 points placed him second to Aub Lawson in the Australian score chart. The series was a whitewash with Australia the victors 7-1. This was by far the best season for the Mittagong Flash who proved he could rise to the occasion as an individual as well as a team man.

Keith's first major success was reported in the Sydney Sunday Herald on 13 January 1952:

'Keith Ryan won his first major speedway title in a dramatic final heat of the Australian three-lap Championship at Sydney Showground last night. Ryan gained a possible 15 points from his five rides to beat Lionel Levy and title holder Jack Parker by two points. Ryan, Levy, Parker, and Australian Test captain Aub Lawson, all had chances of winning the title when they lined up in Heat 20.

Graham Warren: 'He was a sensation . . . he could have been a World Champion'.

'Ryan got out in front of Levy with the English captain slightly behind in third position. By clever riding, Ryan was able to prevent Levy from taking the lead, and Parker seemed unable to pass either man. Levy made a desperate bid in the last lap to catch Ryan, but he was beaten by three lengths.'

The Test series lost momentum in 1953. England sent out a woefully weak team that was thrashed in the reduced series of three matches.

In Febuary Keith was back in Brisbane. The *Brisbane Courier Mail* ran this article on 6 February 1953:

'Four of the world's top speedway riders will make their last appearance at the Exhibition Ground on Saturday night before returning to England for the Coronation season.'

Keith had arranged terms with Glasgow to return for 1953. Back in Sydney Keith boarded the Orontes with the intent of travelling to England. It had been three seasons since he last rode in Britain. On the way to Fremantle he received a cable from the Claremont promoter Ossie Mitcheldon offering two meetings in Perth if he would break his journey and then continue to Britain by air. This he agreed to do.

The following day, 28 February 1953 the papers reported:

'A spectacular debut by Keith Ryan, the international speedway rider, conceding big handicaps, he won the four solo events in which he started.'

With plans to return to Britain, his appearance in Perth at the Claremont track was announced in the West Australian newspaper on the morning of 6 March 1953 as Ryan's farewell appearance before leaving for England by air to ride in the first Division at West Ham.

During his stay in Perth Keith had a change of heart about returning to Glasgow and requested a transfer to a First Division team. The Tigers promptly placed a fee of £600 on his head. A high figure at that time and an indication of his value as a rider.

West Ham took up the offer. Their Aussie riders Jack Young and Cliff Watson were able to verify Keith's Australian form to their management and the deal was struck. As it turned out a family illness wrecked all the plans. Keith never made the trip and returned to Sydney.

With the Test matches against England ending in the 1953-54 Australian season, so did Keith's Test career.

Graham Warren, who was recovering from injury, encouraged Keith to travel overland with him to Adelaide in February 1954, then on to Perth to ride at Claremont. There was mention again of carrying on to England to ride, but that did not happen.

Keith's career was at an end. The sport had also hit lean times worldwide. It was another decade before interest was rekindled with the introduction of the Australia v England Test matches. A new decade of great racing was then enjoyed.

Keith rates as his most admired peers: Jack Parker, Aub Lawson, Lionel Van Praag, Vic Duggan, Max Grosskreutz and Lionel Levy.

After his retirement from racing Keith started a small metal fabrication business manufacturing ornamental gates and fencing. He also kept his hand in making speedway frames. He is still very much interested in the juniors coming through in the sport and is an active member in the Australian Veteran Speedway riders Association being President in 1994 - 95.

On 18 May 2003 Keith had the honour of unveiling the commemorative plaque at the old West Maitland Speedway site in New South Wales where he won the 2-lap Australian Championship on February 9th 1952.

Another notable memory was the presentation of a replica Glasgow Tigers race jacket

Left to right:
Aub Lawson at his spectacular best as a trailer before changing to the foot-forward style. 'He was a great Test partner'.

Most admired. The great Max Grosskreutz leading Jack Parker at Bradford.

Highly rated. Lionel Van Praag (right) and Ray Duggan. Keith 'grew up with Vic and Ray Duggan. Vic had fast motors and was very hard to beat. After Ray's death (in a track accident) Vic ... was lost to the speedway world'.

Top: *Honoured – Keith unveils the plaque at West Maitland speedway where he became the Australian Two Lap Champion.*

Above: *Notable – veteran Australian journalist Peter White presents Keith with a souvenir Glasgow Tigers race jacket.*

in 2010 by AVSRA member Rob Ogilvy.

Keith, now 95, rates his most admired peers as Jack Parker, Aub Lawson, Lionel Van Praag, Vic Duggan, Max Grosskreutz and Lionel Levy. He is forthright in expressing his opinions of the top stars of his day.

Ken le Breton

I regarded Ken as a close friend, we travelled to England together in 1947, although Ken signed for New Cross and was loaned to Newcastle and I was at Glasgow we boarded together for a while. When Ken moved to Ashfield his following was so great that the track died after Ken's passing. He was Ashfield speedway. He was loved by all and would surely have been a World Champion if fate had been kinder to him.

Graham Warren

Graham and I go back to the mudflats at Tempe in 1939, he could have been a World Champion had it not been for the tragic accident in New Zealand when he fractured his skull at the height of his career. He was good looking, popular with the fans, especially at Birmingham where, from 1948 he was a sensation. When Graham was married the whole of the centre of the city of Birmingham came to a halt.

Jack Young

I rode a lot against Youngie, he was such a smooth stylist, he made it look so easy. I do not think we saw the best of jack in Australia, his English seasons were so hectic he relaxed a bit when he got home.

Jack Parker

England's best, he held the Test series together against all odds and was not afraid of officialdom. Mechanically he was brilliant.

He was the master tactician, fair and clean. He rode in more Test matches and championships then any other rider. His farewell Test appearance in Australia saw him go out with a 15 point score at the age of 46.

The pipe smoking English gentleman was a façade, he could be a hell raiser with the best given the opportunity. Sadly Jack's demise was after he was knocked down crossing the road, ironic after a lifetime courting danger with speedway racing.

The speedcar accident at the Showground brought his speedway days to an earlier end otherwise he would have had a few more seasons. When you think that in 1952 Parker went around the Showground at 59.00, a time hard pushed to equal today with all the state of the art equipment.

Aub Lawson

Aub was a great Test partner and a very fair rider. We rode good as a pair and could read each other. I took over from him as Australian captain in 1951.

Vic and Ray Duggan

I grew up with the Duggans, worked with them and rode with them. Vic always had fast motors and was vey hard to beat. Ray's death was a tragedy and Vic was never the same afterwards. His retirement was abrupt and for many years was lost to the speedway world which is understandable. Possibly one of the best who never became a World Champion.

Lionel Van Praag

Lionel was a very tough rider to pass, he was very experieced having started riding in 1926.

He would move out on you if you tried the outside run and was not adverse to kicking your front wheel if you tried the inside.

He always had very fast engines and he knew every trick in the book.

Lionel Levy

A very close friend. We rode together for many seasons. Lionel was also in England in 1947 but could never get to grips with the tracks there. In Australia he was unbeatable.

MY sincere thanks to Tony Webb for his original words for this Keith Ryan appreciation

Chapter 39
DICKY AND SUPERMAX TAKE ON HERR HITLER

AND LOSE... WELL, WHAT DID YOU EXPECT?

SPEEDWAY folklore is a strange and wonderful thing. The trouble is that sometimes – to use a well-known Fleet Street cliché – facts can get in the way of a good story.

Now then, I'll explain. There are two versions of a story about this picture. If I tell both of them to you, you can decide for yourselves which one you prefer.

The picture shows an imposing all-star line-up of dedicated dirt-track heroes. The location is Hamburg in Germany dated 1933. Adolph Hitler, aided by his black shirted thugs, had just begun his spectacular rise to power that was to plunge the world into a new dark age of terror and despair.

However, all that was a few years away, well before the 1939 World Final had to be called off because Herr Hitler's global war broke out and all speedway went into a virtual six year hibernation.

Leading the parade is top Australian international Dicky Case, then with Coventry. On the far right is Ernie Evans, then with Sheffield, and next to him is the one and only Max Grosskreutz (SuperMax) who was then with Belle Vue.

How it all came about, according to contemporary reports, was this: Dicky had amassed a small fortune and, being of an enterprising and entrepreneurial disposition, his thoughts

turned to Germany. He and Max, and what was described as 'some lesser known riders' (which explains why the others in the picture are not named) reopened speedways in Hamburg and other provincial towns. And the crowds rolled up in their thousands.

As detailed in Tom Stenner's book ***Thrilling The Million*** 'the new Hitler regime was all in favour of a manly sport and the Nazi stormtroopers kept order at meetings'. Then there was a change of government policy which decreed that Germany was for Germans and a foreign enterprise should not be supported. Attendances at Dicky and Max's speedways then dwindled to virtual vanishing point.

But Dicky and Max put on one last meeting before being evicted by Hitler's henchmen – an all-star championship with a valuable gold cup as the top prize. Finances by this time were running low so our two intrepid heroes visited a local pawnbroker and acquired – for a considerable sum – a gold cup in the confident certainty that, as they were far superior to any of the other riders, they were sure to win it and be able to return it safely to the pawnbroker. And of course collect the cash they had left as surety.

Unfortunately in the qualifiers Max had engine trouble and Dicky broke a chain as he was about half a lap ahead of the opposition. So the gold cup was won by a German who refused to part with his prize, not even for as many marks as Max and Dicky could muster between them.

The pawnbroker was not taken in by their tale of woe, convinced it was all a plot. It was only by leaving their speedway bikes as security that they avoided arrest.

So, there you have it. As colourful a tale of adventure as you will find in the speedway annals. Unless . . .

If you believe the chronology of some commentators of the day, the Case-Grosskreutz excursion took place in 1931, by which time Hitler had been only a few years out of jail after writing his memoir ***Mein Kampf*** and had still to come to power.

Well, I tell you, it's really your choice which version you prefer. I know which one I'm going for.

The entrepeneur in action. Dick Case whose plot to take the top prize went horribly wrong.

Chapter 40
TO HELLABY AND BACK FOR A COOL MILLION

FARMER'S boy Tommy Bateman started to pursue his dream of speedway stardom at the age of 16 by sliding an old Scott he'd converted round his father's stockyard. It was a 1911 vintage which he'd bought for £2.

He remembered: 'I was given little parental encouragement.' Perhaps his Dad could see what was coming. Tommy crashed, breaking a leg and losing a finger.

In 1929, fit again and undeterred, he entered himself in a meeting at Hellaby, a track near Rotherham. His father went along to watch because, Tommy reckoned, his Dad thought he couldn't do himself much damage on such an ancient steed.

To get to the event he and a friend had to tow the bike 40 miles. He finished third in his first ride and, he said it was completely overshadowed by his second ride. His opponent, he realized, was mounted on 'a rip-snorting, genuine Dirt-Track Douglas'.

He told himself: 'Tommy, this is where you have a real bash.' They were push starts in those days – no taped starting gates – and Tommy said: 'The Scott was a grand starter and I was first round the bend. Seven times that Douggie passed me and seven times I passed him and managed to cross the finishing line two lengths in front. What a thriller.'

He'd qualified for the final, and over-eagerness got the better of him. He crashed. But, he said: 'I managed to remount and finished third.'

It was, he insisted, the greatest ride of his career. Especially when he got his prize money: thirtyfive bob (£1.75p). His weekly wage at a Scunthorpe garage was only 25shillings (£1.25p). 'I felt like a millionaire,' he said.

Tommy's pre-war career took him to Lea Bridge, Nottingham and Hackney, where he helped the team to the 1938 Second Division league championship.

He was to come close to medals again after the war with Sheffield. The Yorkshire side were Northern league runners-up three times between 1946 and 1949 and Tommy was Sheffield's top scorer in 1947 in a team that included the veteran Tommy Allott, Len and Stan Williams and the fast rising Bruce Semmens.

But when Sheffield dropped out of the league in 1950, Tommy went to Newcastle and, though still a high scorer, after a crash at Edinbugh in which he broke a thigh he retired from racing.

After 20 years on the track, he said: 'I shall always look back at that Hellaby meeting and think of my ancient Scott with an affection that no other cinders thrill will ever replace.'

Panoramic powerhouse. The magnificence of The Old Frying Pan pride of the Old Kent Road.

Chapter 41

IN . . . AND OUT . . . OF THE OLD FRYING PAN

This is what Messrs Mockford and Smith left behind. An early speedway race taking place at the unique and packed Crystal Palace with the famed 'Glass Palace' rising over the grandstand in the background.

WHEN London was the powerhouse and Mecca of world speedway the neat little track and stadium at New Cross, just off the fabled Old Kent Road, was one of the most glittering arenas in the sport's firmament.

And from this magnificent panorama taken in 1935 you can see why it was chosen as the location for the seminal speedway film *Once A Jolly Swagman* which starred Sir Dirk Bogarde, Renee Asherson, Bonar Coleano, Thora Hird, Moira Lister, Bill Owen, Syd James (and several authentic speedway riders who doubled for the stars).

The speedway world knew it as The Frying Pan – because it was the smallest track in the land at 262 yards. Track width was 30ft, stadium capacity was 30,000. In 1935 Tom Farndon set a track record of 59.6 seconds – the first time a speedway rider had completed four laps from a clutch start in under one minute.

In 1939 Arthur Atrkinson reduced the time to 58.0 seconds and by the time New Cross ceased to exist in 1963 the record was 57.0 held by Ove Fundin, who confessed to loving the track, but by then the length had gone up 16 yards to 278 yards.

The story and the glory days began, and also ended, with two men, both entrepreneurs, but so different that their natural talents complimented each other perfectly. They were Fred Mockford, a born showman whose middle name was said to be 'Baloney', and the quiet, unassuming Cecil Smith, who in 1928 had persuaded the owners of the iconic Crystal Palace to allow the dynamic duo to introduce motorcycle path racing in the grounds of the south London complex.

By 1933, the Palace was in decline, only the path racing and the newly emerged sporting sensation of dirt-track racing were pulling in the crowds. So the Palace trustees hiked the rent and refused to allow Messrs Mockford and Smith to install floodlighting. Fred and Cecil were having none of that and took their business elsewhere . . . to the little greyhound stadium at New Cross.

A couple of years later the main Palace building, a

The team taking up residence at New Cross in 1934. Standing from the left: Harry Shepherd, who helped devise the modern speedway taped starting gate, Roy Dook, Stan Greatrex and George Newton. Sitting: Joe Francis, Tom Farndon, Fred Mockford, Ron Johnson and Nobby Key.

glittering structure of cast iron and the greatest area of glass ever seen, was destroyed in a devastating fire.

Having decamped in the nick of time to the Old Kent Road, the Mockford-Smith partnership bristled with ideas and innovations. New Cross rivalled the mighty Wembley with its speedway workshop facilities. Mockford had all the team machines distinctly copper plated.

The bikes were first heard at the new stadium behind Hornshay Street SE15 when New Cross beat West Ham 32 – 21 in a National League (First Division) match in front of 15,000 fans.

That same year Mockford replaced the irritating and unpredictable flag starts by introducing the taped starting gate, forerunner of the type still in use today. It had been

And a view of the stadium from the air. In the background over the back fence is the old Milwall football ground, and in the bottom right hand corner, the tips of the gardens of the houses in Hornshay Street.

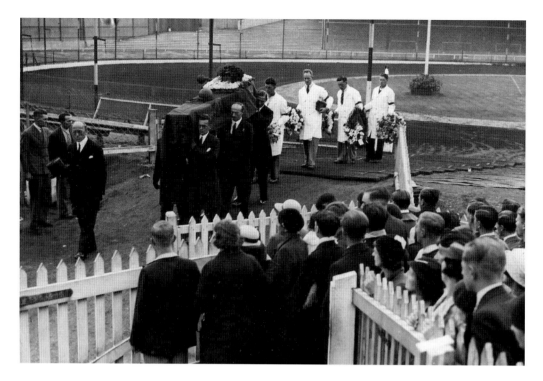

Tragedy. The coffin of Tom Farndon, New Cross's star rider and virtually the world's best at the time, is carried solemnly and with great ceremony from the centre green where it had lain in state following his fatal accident. Thousands attended the stadium to pay their respects to their fallen idol.

developed and built by rider Harry Shepherd and his mechanic Alf Smith.

Tragedy struck when New Cross's major star, British Champion Tom Farndon – then undoubtedly the world's best and the sport's most outstanding performer – was killed in a shocking crash with team mate Ron Johnson in an unimportant second half race on the eve of the 1935 Star Final at Wembley for which he was favourite. Farndon is the only rider to have died in an accident at New Cross.

In spite of what was a dreadful loss, Mockford and Smith did not wail, gnash their teeth and demand assistance, they went out and helped themselves by enticing to London America's glamorous Milne brothers, Jack and Cordy, who had been enjoying astonishing success in Australia.

The trouble was the speedway bureaucrats didn't take too kindly to the Mockford-Smith enterprise and took Cordy away, allocating him to the weaker Hackney because it was ruled New Cross would have been far too strong had they been allowed to keep both the Milnes.

Within two seasons Mockford and Smith were able to add a crowd-pulling World Champion to their little citadel when Jack Milne won the 1937 title at Wembley. As if to

Star turn: Dirk Bogarde in speedway leathers and astride a bike before the cameras set up on the New Cross first bend. He is being directed by Jack Lee. Asked about his experience years later Bogarde said he could remember no details except that he 'was petrified'.

underline their astuteness, Cordy was favourite for the 1939 World Championship, but Adolph Hitler put paid to that by starting a war a few days before the Final which was cancelled.

The 1938 season was New Cross's best pre-war year when they won the National League title by five points from West Ham. A decade later they did it again when they finished as champions ahead of Harringay.

In 1947, amid much publicity New Cross signed Australian Ken LeBreton whose eye-catching gimmick was to ride in all-white leathers on a white bike and earn him the title The White Ghost. A week before he was due to make his debut he was introduced to the Old Kent Road crowd on the centre green dressed smartly in business suit with a bowler hat and carrying a tightly rolled umbrella. It was never disclosed whether it was all LeBreton's idea or if showman Mockford had put him up to it. LeBreton was not a success at New Cross and soon departed for Second Division Newcastle, where he later became a huge star.

Post war speedway at New Cross began an almost imperceptible decline with an accident to the man who was then the unchallenged idol of the Old Kent Road faithful, Ron Johnson, rightly described as a superstar. He suffered a fractured skull in a crash at Wimbledon in 1949.

Ron was never the same force again, though making several comeback attempts. He ended with him finishing a pathetic shadow of the brilliant speedway practitioner who had soared to second place behind Vic Duggan at Wembley in the previous year's Speedway Riders Championship Final, the last great competition before the official World Championship was reintroduced in 1949.

As Johnson lost his way, so did New Cross and indeed the sport as a whole. Smith departed and in 1953 Mockford, once more the victim of speedway bureaucracy, was refused permission to include Sweden's Olle Nygren in the side. He turned off the gas under The Old Frying Pan, pulled the Rangers out of the league and closed the place down.

Later, speedway did return, promoted by Mockford's bitter rival Johnnie Hoskins. But even with secure financial backing Johnnie failed to lure back the crowds and at the end of 1961 he too quit the Old Kent Road. Former rider Wally Mawdsley then entered a team in the Provincial League but that promotion folded midway through the 1963 season. The final match was on 2 August when visiting Poole won 41 – 37.

Eventually Lewisham council bought the land from owners British Rail and in March 1974 the demolition men moved in and knocked down the old stadium which was turned into parkland. It signalled the end of an era that for more than 40 years had been very much a part of the life of south London.

And the Rangers didn't do too badly over those decades: One World Champion, two league titles, two London Cups, an AC-U Cup and a Spring Cup.

The Old Frying Pan is now a recreation ground, and its shape can still be made out if you look hard enough.

The real thing. Wearing the Swagman team's Cobra race jacket for filming, Ron Howes, who was then with West Ham, was one of the genuine riders who doubled for some of the actors in the action scenes.

Nominated. A Swagman poster listing the stars and trumpeting that the film was BAFTA nominated.

The end. This is what became of that splendid arena – deserted, abandoned, overgrown, derelict, unwanted and pathetic, before it was turned into a recreation area.

Chapter 42
THE MERRIEST MONARCHS

WELL, they look happy enough. Which is perhaps why one commentator referred to them as the Merry Monarchs. Though why they should be so pleased with themselves is a mystery because they had just lost Jack Young, who had swept like a tornado through not only Scottish but world speedway.

This is seven-eighths of the 1952 Second Division Edinburgh team, because in those days there were eight riders in a side. Young had taken himself off to First Division West Ham for a then record £3,500 transfer fee having astounded the entire sport by becoming World Champion at Wembley the previous year. He would, even more astoundingly, do it again before the 1952 season was out.

But the satisfied look of this line-up, pictured at Old Meadowbank, could be explained by the fact that around about that time they were riding before regular near capacity crowds of 22,000. No wonder they were described, quaintly, as 'thistle land's most all round attractive team' against the three other Scottish tracks, at Ashfield, Glasgow White City and Motherwell. It could be thought that the Monarchs went on to even higher things. They eventually left Edinburgh for Coatbridge who in turn became the revived Wembley Lions of the Seventies, Bert 'Haggis' Harkins and all.

They were masterminded by the gent in the hat and natty suiting, pre-war New Cross star Clem Mitchell, who made the briefest of comebacks until informed by the Control Board he couldn't be a rider and the manager.

The merriest of Monarchs are, from the left, Jimmy Cox, Harry Darling, Eddie Lack, Bob Mark (on bike), Don Cuppleditch, Harold Fairhurst, Clem Mitchell (Manager), Dick Campbell.

Missing is Johnny Green who, in the 1980s, fell by the wayside because he apparently strayed from the straight and narrow.

Chapter 43
KENNY AND BRUCE

SPEEDWAY'S MOST DYNAMIC OF DUOS

YOU wouldn't suspect, would you, that these two happy chappies were anything other than the best of buddies?

This was, of course, before it all kicked off. They are England's Kenny Carter (LADA) and America's Bruce Penhall (BEL-RAY), undoubtedly, one of the most potent and dynamic duos in the history of speedway racing – bar none.

Their track confrontations in the 1970s and 1980s brought about the same frisson of expectation as did the clashes in the 1930s between Belle Vue's England star Frank 'El Diablo Rojo' Varey and Australia's Lionel 'Hard Man' Van Praag of Wembley, the first official World Champion. Frank once said: 'We emptied the bars when we were on the track.'

It was the same with Kenny who had 'I hate Americans' badges made, and Juicy 'Glamour Boy' Brucie. Their festering animosity all came to a final viciously explosive confrontation in the Los Angeles Coliseum in 1982 when the prize they were fighting for – literally – was speedway's supreme title, World Champion.

Bruce was the reigning title holder, having won the year before at Wembley. Kenny had finished fifth and for some time had considered that the World Championship was his by right. It was well known that his uncompromising character was such that 'he just couldn't stand to lose'.

They came from entirely opposite backgrounds. Carter, from Halifax, was the stereotypical blunt, Yorkshireman: fearless, outspoken and always ready to stand up for

Kenny and Bruce – two young men laughing at the world, their differing destinies and untold success ahead of them . . . it could have been so different . . . it could have been this good.

The cataclysmic Heat 14 at the Los Angeles Coliseum in the 1982 World Final. Although you see only three riders leaving the tapes – England's Peter Collins nearest camera, Bruce Penhall, centre, and Kenny Carter, outside, there was a fourth rider in the heat, Australia's Phil Crump. Kenny and Bruce were both unbeaten after three rides and they were so concerned with concentrating on each other they allowed Peter Collins to take the lead followed by Crump and both rode off into the distance. After a lot of bumping into each other, which appeared to be tantamount to fighting on speedway machines, Kenny and Bruce passed Crump on lap two.

Moment of truth. Bruce gets under Kenny going into the first bend on lap three. He then had the advantage and could begin to dictate the race. Exiting the turn Bruce rode a wide line and Kenny, on his outside, came down. The race was stopped and Kenny was excluded as being the cause of the stoppage.

himself. He was not universally popular with other riders, even his England team mates. One reason was that he insisted on wearing the No.1 race jacket.

Kenny's father Mal stood no nonsense. Former top rider Eric Boothroyd, who ran Halifax, remembered him being asked to see the 16-year-old Kenny ride. He said: 'Kenny came up to us and said: "I can't race, I've fallen off and broken my wrist." Mal told him: "Don't be a soft little bugger, get on your bike and show us what you can do. Eric's come specially to see you." '

How rough, bluff and tough is that?

Bruce was the stereotypical bronzed beach boy who had the privilege of being brought up in California, enjoying all the surfing, sunshine and glamorous razzmatazz that went with it . . . the Golden Boy from the Golden State. And from virtually the time he joined Cradley Heath in 1978 success seemed to not only follow him around, but thrust itself upon him – especially when it came to the ladies.

It is ironic, but instead of their bitter rivalry it could have been so very different. They might easily have been team mates and colleagues at Halifax, having to look out for each other and help each other on the track. Eric Boothroyd said that he had done a post World Final deal with Bruce in 1977 for him to finish the season with Halifax, 'but Bruce's girlfriend decided she wanted to go back home so he reluctantly ducked out'.

The eventual outcome is well documented. Bruce went out in a blaze of glory as World Champion for the second successive time amid the celebratory fireworks in the Los Angeles Coliseum. Kenny had to be removed from the track after protesting furiously at his exclusion from Heat 14 after his clash with Bruce.

The aftermath. Furious, and feeling discriminated against, Kenny at first refused to accept his exclusion and eventually had to be escorted from the starting gate by security heavies. Back in the pits, with his mechanic on one side and on the other his manager, multi-World Champion Ivan Mauger, who was also co-promoter of the meeting, harsh words were directed at referee Torre Kittilesen. But Kenny stayed excluded, the race was rerun won by Penhall with Collins second and Crump third. Bruce became World Champion for the second consecutive time and Kenny was fifth.

Then Bruce quit speedway on the rostrum for a career – a very short career - in television and films.

Kenny said at the time: 'I think that's lousy . . . if you become World Champion you should do something for the sport.'

Perhaps because he never got over what was denied him, the thing he wanted above all else – the World Championship – and any real or imagined domestic difficulties, Kennys shot and killed his wife Pam and then turned the gun on himself.

How tough, rough and tragic is that?

Chapter 44
A COUPLE OF SWELLS

WELL, as some joker might say: 'It's a hell of a job, but someone has to do it.' And then, looking at these two you have to ask yourself: Why?

This was BDD – before Dirt Deflectors – of course. You won't recognise these two protagonists who appear to have been enjoying a mud bath – or is it an old fashioned cinders bath? So I'll reveal their identities straight away.

On the left is Bobby Blake and on the right is Ray Tauser. Now I am well aware that the modern enthusiast may not readily call to mind their names. After all they were stars whose twinkle faded long ago in the speedway mists of time.

Bobby Blake, an Australian who came over with the original pioneers, could be seen in the early days strutting his spectacular stuff at the old London White City stadium. He won the New South Wales Championship in 1930, a title later to be won by many of the greats including Bluey Wilkinson, Tiger Stevenson, Jack Milne, Max Grosskreutz and Vic Duggan.

He rode for Australia in the home Tests of 1932, but four years later was killed in a practice crash at the Maroubra track which at the inquest was condemned by the coroner as 'unsafe and should not be used by anyone'. His real name was Robert Coombs and Blake was his 'professional' name.

Ray Tauser, described as 'a clever American, was the biggest star from the USA of the late Twenties and early Thirties alongside the iconic Lloyd 'Sprouts' Elder, Art Pechar and Cecil Brown.

Ray, known as 'Terror' Tauser, from Portland, Oregon, was that good he was reported to have been contracted to appear at 60 speedway tracks in Britain – a mind-boggling number compared with today. He followed up considerable success in Australia by winning the 1931 Star Championship at Wembley, then the equivalent of a World Championship.

The Star's Speedway Correspondent reported: 'Ray Tauser created a sensation when he won the Star Trophy last night in competition with the finest speedway exponents in the world.' They included Vic Huxley, Jack Parker, Colin Watson, Ron Johnson and Frank Arthur.

Ray rode for Wimbledon but under employment laws in operation then was expelled from Britain and had to return to America where he continued racing in California during the late 1930s. He was eventually inducted into the AMA Motorcycle Hall Of Fame.

Chapter 45

YOU'VE EITHER GOT, OR YOU HAVEN'T GOT, STYLE

AND THESE ACES CERTAINLY HAVE IT

THIS looks intriguing. And not even a cinder, a bike or a suit of leathers in sight.

At first glance it is a real sober gathering of respectful young men hanging on every word of sage advice being handed out by the gentleman in the country-style tweed jacket who is ruminating on that old fashioned pipe.

But you know how appearances can be deceptive . . .

The pipe-smoking luminary was, when the picture was taken, a bit of a speedway elder statesman of some 40 years whose racing reputation went right back to the beginning of dirt track racing in this country.

He is Walter (Wally) Hull a distinguished Belle Vue Ace of yesteryear who first took to the track in 1928 at the famous meeting on the Audenshaw trotting circuit just outside Manchester which was staged a mere three weeks after High Beech.

When things really got going he graced several pre-war London teams including Wimbledon, Lea Bridge and Hackney Wick, besides Sheffield, and was a member of the England side which defeated Australia 56 – 39 in the second Test of the historic first series in 1930. There was another tilt at the antipodeans in the fourth Test, again at Belle Vue, which ran out another England win at 51 – 45.

Wally played a significant part in the dominant Belle Vue steamroller that monopolised most of the club honours in the mid-Thirties right up to the war. He didn't ride again immediately after the war when league racing returned in 1946 but made a comeback in 1947, once again in Aces colours, helping them win the National Trophy for the seventh time. Two years later he became team manager at Sheffield then promoted by Belle Vue boss Alice Hart.

He has been described as 'tall and gentlemanly, a demeanour that may have influenced his youthful companions here. Who are – or were at the time – Belle Vue wannabees Dent Oliver (left) and Louis Lawson (right), both of whom went on to greater things, Lawson to World No.3 in 1949. The odd one out is Oliver 'Laughing Boy' Hart of Odsal, virtually the very last of the old time leg-trailers and one of the sport's most spectacular crowd pleasers.

Every one of them is wearing a smart suit together with an immaculately knotted tie. Well groomed I think would be the term to describe them as they present a high profile image to the public that can bring only credit to the sport.

Something you don't see often in this super-casual, let-it-all-hang-out age. Or should that be super-scruffy, unkempt, tattooed, don't-give-a-damn age?

Chapter 46
GOODEN'S EXOTIC OLDSMOBILE COMES TO THE AID OF ENGLAND

THIS is how the elite of world speedway travelled to important meetings when they hit the big time fifty – sixty years ago.

If they were lucky.

Otherwise they hitched their bike on to a special bracket fixed to the back of the sort of cars you can see parked against that wall. Or they loaded up the machinery onto the slightly more up-market convenience of a trailer such as the one out in the road.

You will have observed It is all a long way from the luxurious, lavishly fitted out motor homes in which your modern Grand Prix star now rolls up to meetings in what doubles as a mobile workshop and an entertainment centre so that he may offer hospitality to his numerous sponsors.

The amazing set-up before you is courtesy of Vic *'Mr Philanthropic'* Gooden, sometime rider, sometime promoter and once described as 'perhaps the most rip-roaring, outrageous and colourful personality in speedway' by the man who had seen and knew them all, the sport's most outstanding publicist the late Dave Lanning.

Vic Gooden was never even remotely a World Champion. In fact he never really progressed higher than Third Division standard as a rider. But he did hold the world record for pouring money into speedway to enable the sport to simply survive. It was once said that he was earning £1,000 a week selling cars when brain surgeons were getting that a year.

That magnificent machine is Vic's Oldsmobile . . . and the occasion is an England tour party about to set off from team manager Mr Gooden's used car yard in East London. The group, from right to left, includes Peter Craven, Dick Bradley, Ken McKinlay, Mike Broadbank and George White, with Wimbledon manager Ted Brine leaning on the car boot and Vic bending over the trailer. As you can see, such a stellar selection of speedway

superstars has attracted a massive fan following – two curious housewives and a little boy across the street.

The big question must be: who took the picture? Because, on the left, standing there all casual-like with his hands in his pockets, intrigued by what is going on, is speedway's snapper supreme Alf *(Est 1947)* Weedon. The only clue is the words on the back of the original print: L.E. Ellis, 25 Hillcot House, Clarissa Street, London E8 – that's not a million miles away from Hackney's old Waterden Road Stadium.

The Oldsmobile is one of Vic's legendary fleet that caused many a jaw to drop around the speedway tracks during that period, the late Fifties. And if film buffs are hearing the faint ringing of bells, the car is the same model used by Stanley Baker in the 1958 movie *Hell Drivers*.

Born in Huntingdon in 1921, Vic emerged from the seedy Damon Runyonesque world of London's East End where he had earned a few quid as a bouncer at one of the area's most notorious

And this is Vic Gooden's other exotic car (below) – or one of them – his prized Rolls-Royce (note the personalised registration plate, VG 15), and, during his other life as a genuine speedway rider, in action for Rayleigh.

dance halls, to become one of the long line of early post-war graduates of the Rye House training school.

He joined Rayleigh in 1948 and was, with team mate Ron Howes, one of the real speedway riders who doubled for stars in the film *Once A Jolly Swagman*.

He had an exotic taste in those spectacular cars, from Oldsmobiles to Rolls-Royces, in which he delighted in doing 130mph on the Southend Arterial Road.

If he was never world class as a rider, he never won much as a promoter either, at Rayleigh, Poole or Ipswich, except respect. But he was world class at being a cavalier character with a carefree attitude to life and the living of it until his death in 2010 aged 89.

Chapter 47
A PRIDE OF WEMBLEY LIONS

A FINER body of men you won't encounter anywhere. It's an interesting turnout for a number of reasons. There is an interloper for one thing, someone who really shouldn't be there at all.

There are two clues. One is the rampant lion on the sweater of the chap leading the line on the left. The other is in the person who has almost – but not quite – managed to hide himself at the very back of the pack.

Actually this lot should be termed a Pride . . . a Pride of Lions. Wembley Lions 1931-1932 vintage, being put through their paces by the trainer striding out at the front – whose name unfortunately is not known.

But leading his Wembley side round their home track to make sure the boys keep in trim is captain Colin Watson, who had been in it from the very first official meeting at High Beech in 1928. Following him, and looking as though they are actually enjoying the experience, are Jack Ormston, Colin Stewart and Reg Bounds.

In the right hand lane are George Greenwood, New Zealander Wally Kilmister, Harry Whitfield, Charlie Sheldon, behind him Gordon Byers, and bringing up the rear Lionel Van Praag.

Almost hidden between Sheldon and Byers is the man tasked with making the Wembley Lions mighty, the Old Windbag himself Johnnie S. Hoskins, who always claimed to be responsible for creating the entire sport in the first place but could not by any stretch of the imagination claim to be a speedway rider.

Of course, the entire escapade could have been a gigantic publicity stunt. Watson, at the time, was a contender to beat Wimbledon's Vic Huxley for the ('unofficial') World Championship. He didn't. And when speedway got around to staging an official competition, it was Van Praag who confounded them all by winning the first genuine world title in 1936.

Hoskins, with the connivance of Wembley boss Arthur Elvin's business brain, had rescued the Lions from disaster when it was thought that metropolitan crowds would never travel so far out of London to make the enterprise profitable. He fashioned them into a super successful club with a trophy haul the envy of speedway and a supporters' club that was filling those terraces you see in the background with 60,000 paying customers a week.

Around this time West Ham speedway found itself in financial difficulties so Elvin took the track over and installed Hoskins to manage it. Which he did, once again, with outstanding success even 'stealing' Elvin's interval attractions idea by staging eccentric and exotic events of his own for the Custom House faithful and becoming known as the Admiral Of Barking Creek.

SPEEDWAY SWINGS AT THE ALBERT HALL

SHOULD I tell you that the Speedway Riders Association once hired London's Royal Albert Hall for its annual ball, packed it out with fans who danced the night away to two of the very best swing bands in the land and were entertained with a cabaret starring a Windmill Girl, a top singing star and the nation's leading comedian . . . you probably wouldn't believe me, would you?

Well it did.

It was all in aid of the Speedway Riders Benevolent Fund and, by all accounts, it was a really sumptuous affair. There was dancing to top broadcasting bandleaders Eric Winstone and Billy Ternent plus a star-studded cabaret which included Anita D'Ray one of the scantily clad girls from the notoriously glorious Windmill Theatre, American jazz singer Adelaide Hall and top British comedian 'Cheerful' Charlie Chester.

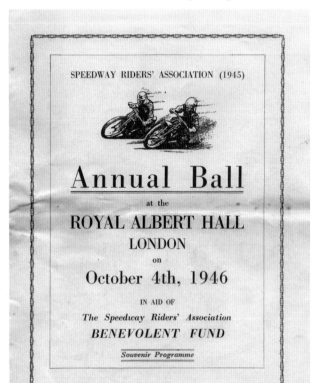

SPEEDWAY RIDERS' ASSOCIATION (1945)

Annual Ball

at the

ROYAL ALBERT HALL

LONDON

on

October 4th, 1946

IN AID OF

The Speedway Riders' Association

BENEVOLENT FUND

Souvenir Programme

The whole thing took place in October 1946 when full-time racing resumed after the war, at the end of the most successful season speedway racing has ever known. Leading journalist Len Steed informed readers in the event's programme that six million people paid to see speedway that year. And there were only twelve tracks in the entire country. Six million people, wrote Steed, who have turned speedway into a national sport rivalling Association Football.

It was a time when world class speedway took place every night of the week in London, and at weekends the show moved out of town to Manchester and Bradford. Attendance figures were staggering: Wembley were top with 1,211,355, West Ham were next with 919,927; Bradford 600,987. Those were National (Premiership) League figures. Even Northern (Championship) League Birmingham attracted 493,862 and Norwich 436,222.

Riders? How much were they paid? Well, stars of GP standard in those days were on £1.10p a start and £1.10p a point, so they refused to sign their contracts until they got a rise. They were given one: 20p extra a point. A rider then at the top of his profession who scored the maximum possible of 12 points in an ordinary league match could go home with the princely sum of £15.60 for his night's work risking life and limb.

How much did it cost the terrace fan to get in? Most expensive was Wembley at 37.5p for the opening meeting on May 9. For a child it cost 3 pence-three-farthings (ask your grandfather what a farthing was) at some tracks.

Were the riders getting a fair deal? As they say: You do the maths. Ben Fund secretary/treasurer at the time, Ivor Pole, wrote in the programme: 'A low annual premium pays a rider £1,000 in the event of losing limbs, eyes or being killed. It also allows for a £10 weekly benefit should a rider be injured and unable to continue racing.'

These days, instead of hiring the Albert Hall, the sport lays on an annual meeting, the Ben Fund Bonanza, to raise money. Ivor Pole's modern equivalent, Paul Ackroyd reveals: 'In 2014 the Fund assisted 40 Riders and 11 disabled ex-riders. The money spent on this was £81,000 compared to £80,000 in 2013. So far 22 riders in 2015, have received assistance and we have spent £30,000.'

Chapter 49
BOOM TIME !

AND WILL MAKES THE MOST OF IT

NOW here's a hectic encounter for you. The picture dates from the time when speedway was re-awakening and had assumed a real position of importance in the nation's thirst for thrills, entertainment and distraction from six years of all-out war.

It was at the dawn of the biggest boom in the sport's history, and something must have been going very right because when this picture was taken West Ham were pulling in 58,000 paying customers a week to Custom House Stadium in London's Docklands. This action wasn't taking place at West Ham, though, it was at the Odsal Stadium Bradford which had been newly-opened by that old West Ham firebrand Johnnie S. Hoskins.

To give you some idea of the crowd speedway was attracting to Odsal every Saturday night, take a look at the picture showing the Bradford first bend.

The main picture is Heat 4 on Monday 12 August 1946, and white lining it with a vengeance is Will Lowther, then the captain of Glasgow in the Northern (Championship) League, whose form that year had been little short of sensational. So determined had Will been to became a speedway rider that when offered a trial at Bristol in 1936 he slept in a barn on the overnight trip south from his Gateshead home.

About to make a pass on his outside is Malcolm Craven of National (Premiership) League West Ham, commonly known as Cackle because of his raucous laugh. Behind them is home man Stan Beardsall and somewhere out of the picture is Fred 'Friar' Tuck at the time also with Odsal.

Behind the action was tragedy. The meeting was a benefit for the family of Albert Rosenfeld, a Bradford rider who had been killed in a previous accident at the track. The incident was one of several which earned Odsal a bad name at the time and resulted in the home team demanding alterations to make the circuit safer.

This was a star-spangled event. Among the really big names that day were England's No.1 and Belle Vue captain Jack Parker, future World Champion Tommy Price of Wembley, Geoff Pymar of New Cross, West Ham captain Eric Chitty and Birmingham skipper Phil 'Tiger' Hart.

The result of the pictured Heat 4: It was won by Malcolm Craven with Fred Tuck second, Will Lowther third and Stan Beardsall fourth. But, according to the the match report the most exciting race turned out to be Heat 18 when Bradford's top two, captain Alec Statham and Ron Clarke, met with 12 points each. 'Statham, with superb white line riding, just managed to snatch victory from Clarke.'

It earned him a 50 guinea trophy presented to commemorate the memory of local JP and Member of Parliament Joe Hepworth.

Chapter 50
BOTTOMS UP

WHEN the man who ruled Wembley, Sir Arthur Elvin, agreed to reopen the Empire Stadium to top flight speedway in 1946 he decided that he would no longer tolerate the whims and often outrageous fortunes demanded by some of the big names from overseas.

Biggest of them all, Australia's Lionel Van Praag decided not to return to austerity-ridden Britain anyway that first year. Neither did his fellow countryman Andy Menzies, Dane Morian Hansen or New Zealander Wally Kilmister.

The great Frank Charles was dead, George Greenwood had retired, Malcolm Craven went to West Ham and so did Aub Lawson. With only the promising pre-war talent of Tommy Price, and the solid George Wilks, Elvin really didn't have a team worthy of the top flight – and a weak Wembley was unthinkable. He had chosen from the 1946 rider pool to lead the Lions only Bill Kitchen of the pre-war Belle Vue colossus.

Sir Arthur summoned his speedway manager, the shrewd Alec Jackson, and told him to find a team of totally British riders. When Jackson said that there just weren't any British riders to be had. Elvin retorted: 'Well make some.'

Which is what Jackson did. The edict gave rise to the famous Rye House Wembley practice sessions. A later graduate, the future double World Champion Fred Williams, described the aspiring speedway stars who took part as 'a rough looking lot of herberts. A load of nutters. There was blood and gore everywhere'.

Jackson must have spotted something in one, Alf Bottoms, because a Wembley contract followed and the 28-year-old Alf found himself in the 1946 Lions National (Premiership) League championship winning side.

Alf, born in fashionable Kensington, was typical of the Jackson talent for discovering talent and just one example of how he thrust young men like Alf in at the deep end to perform in front of the massive crowds that followed speedway then. Real stars such as Split Waterman, Bill Gilbert and Fred Williams were to follow.

Alf Bottoms proved to be one of the discoveries of the year. With a match average of a shade over 6 points in a side that included Bill Kitchen, George Wilks, Tommy Price, Bob

Wells and other Jackson discoveries such as Charlie May, Bill Gilbert, Roy Craighead and Bronco Wilson. The side, said the speedway commentators of the day, was severely underestimated by Jackson.

But a setback was waiting for Alf In 1947. He was struck down with a kidney complaint and had one removed. He appeared in only two league matches for Wembley and his average plummeted to just three.

The following year he was sent to Third Division Southampton amid protests that he should not be allowed to ride at that level because he was too good.

His critics were proved right when he became almost unbeatable, turning in 52 appearances for Southampton scoring 35 maximums and 635 points for an average of over 11.

He is pictured leading the Southampton team of 1948.

From the left they are: Bert Croucher, Cecil Bailey, Tom Oakley, Bob Oakley, Jimmy Squib, Frank Goulden, Alf on the bike, Jimmy Baxter (promoter), Alf Kaines, Bill Griffiths, George Bason.

Unsurprisingly Alf was recalled to Wembley the next year where he rode as a reserve and helped the Lions to win two more successive league titles.

But his passion for cars led to tragedy and he died in a car crash in Luxembourg in 1951 at the age of 32.

Chapter 51
SOLVED: THE STRANGE CASE OF THE VICTORY CUP

WE have a bit of a unique speedway mystery here for you, folks. And we appealled for any fans to come forward to solve it.

First, let me put you in the picture . . . if you'll pardon the pun. The action is from New Cross and the date it was captured was 27 June 1945. That's right, 1945.

The name of the photographer is not recorded, but whoever it was reports: 'A record crowd attended New Cross speedway last night when racing was resumed after an interval of six years. Many thousands were turned away. The picture shows W. Plant leading L. Wotton in Heat 7 of the Victory Cup.'

If memory serves my correctly, there were one or two Victory Cups around at that time. And why not, indeed? The big headline for June 1945 was: *Britain Resounds To Victory Celebrations*, and beneath we were told: 'Suddenly it *(the war)* is all over and Britons have taken to the streets to celebrate victory.'

Many of them took to the terraces at New Cross by the look of it. And by diving back into speedway's dim and distant archives we uncovered a few more details about that celebratory meeting. But not all . . .

To begin with it was a stella line-up, packed with star names and made up of virtually all the regulars who soldiered on at the famous 'We Never Closed' Belle Vue meetings throughout the war years.

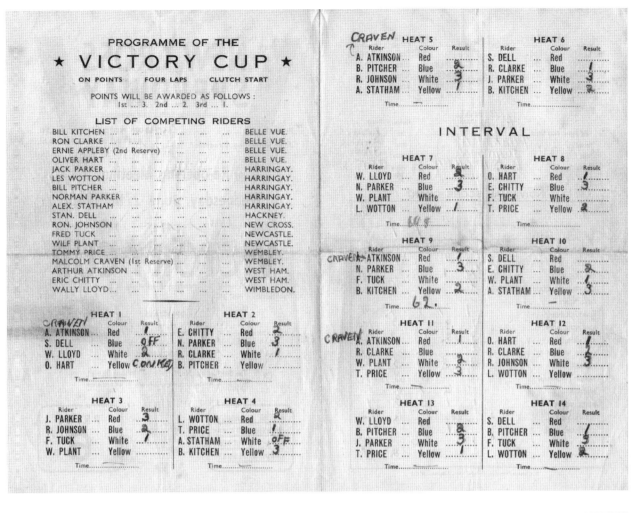

HEAT 15

Rider	Colour	Result
W. LLOYD	Red	1
E. CHITTY	Blue	
B. KITCHEN	White	2
R. JOHNSON	Yellow	

Time......

HEAT 16

Rider	Colour	Result
O. HART	Red	2
N. PARKER	Blue	
J. PARKER	White	
A. STATHAM	Yellow	3

Time......

FINAL

	Rider	Colour	Result
First Highest Point Scorer	PARKER J	Red	FIRST
Second	PARKER N	Blue	SECOND
Third	JOHNSON	White	THIRD
Fourth	B. KITCHEN	Yellow	OFF

Time......

INDIVIDUAL SCORE CHART

RIDER	RACE 1	2	3	4	TOTAL
ATKINSON, ARTHUR	3	—	1	1	5
APPLEBY, ERNIE (2nd Reserve)					
CHITTY, ERIC	2	3	2	1	8
CLARKE, RON	1	1	2		4
CRAVEN, MALCOLM (1st Reserve)					
DELL, STAN	1		1	2	5
HART, OLIVER	2	3	2	3	10
JOHNSON, RON	3	2	3	2	10
KITCHEN, BILL	2		2		4
LLOYD, WALLY					
PARKER, JACK	3	3	3	3	12
PARKER, NORMAN	3	2	3	3	11
PITCHER, BILL		2	1	2	5
PRICE, TOMMY	1	1	2	3	7
PLANT, WILF			2		2
STATHAM, ALEX.		1	3		4
TUCK, FRED	1		3		4
WOTTON, LES.	3		1	1	5

St. Clements Press, Ltd., Portugal Street, Kingsway, W.C.2

There were the Parker brothers, Jack and Norman, Malcolm Craven, Wally Lloyd, Stan Dell, Oliver Hart, Eric Chitty, Ron Clarke, Bill Pitcher, Ron Johnson, Fred Tuck, Wilf Plant, Bill Kitchen, Les Wotton, Tommy Price and Alec Statham, with Ernie Appleby a reserve who never got a ride. As far as we know.

I say as far as we know because only 16 heats were recorded, as you can see from the reproduced programme details. Some riders are credited with three rides and some with four. The individual score sheet seems a little erratic as well. No one seemed to know whether the meeting conformed to the classic 20-heat championship formula. The question of a final had four question marks alongside it, so we didn't know if there *was* a final.

Anyway, the picture shows W (Wilf) Plant leading L (Les) Wotton in, as we have seen, Heat 7. What the pictures does not show is the other riders in the race: Norman Parker, who was the winner, and Wally Lloyd, who was second. Les Wotton eventually overtook Wilf Plant to finish third.

Amazingly the times for all the recorded heats are above 61 seconds – the fastest was 61.4 posted by Jack Parker in Heat 3. Tom Farndon of New Cross in beating Wimbledon's Vic Huxley in the second leg of their British Championship match in 1934 went round four laps of the Old Kent Road track's 262 yards in 59 3/5ths seconds.

The top scorers at New Cross that day in June 1945 were the Parker brothers with nine points – three straight wins – each. Ron Johnson was next on 8 from three rides with Eric Chitty and Bill Kitchen on 7 from three rides.

But, Malcolm Craven, Stan Dell, Ron Clarke, Bill Pitcher, Fred Tuck, Wilf Plant, Les Wotton and Tommy Price all had four rides each.

So . . . a solution was needed to the mystery of the incomplete meeting . . . or was it incomplete? Maybe the celebrations got out of hand and they all just decided to call it a day and go merrily on their way.

The mystery could have been the speedway equivalent of the famous riddle of the Mary Celeste, a boat found drifting and abandoned in mid-Atlantic in 1872, which has baffled mariners for almost 150 years. Our Victory Cup day at New Cross may never have been solved.

Or so I thought . . .

***

IT seems you can always rely on speedway people to come up with the goods. The ink was hardly dry on my intriguingly Victory Cup mystery when, as if by magic, the mystery was solved.

Kevin Gray was first out of the traps and sent me an e-mail explaining: 'The meeting was a 16 heat format with the four highest scoring riders in the final.

'The final line-up was Jack Parker in red, Norman Parker in blue , Ron Johnson in white and Bill Kitchen in yellow. And they finished in that order. Winner's time: 61.6'

Kevin's e-mail was followed up with another from my colleague John Somerville who sent a copy of the programme (pictured) confirming the results – except that whoever filled in the programme, as you can see, had Norman Parker's heat results slightly mixed. In the programme Norman Parker is down as finishing second in his second ride. In fact he won that from Wally Lloyd, Les Wotton and Wilf Plant as we reported above. The scorer has Norman winning his last ride, but he lost that to brother Jack in the grand final.

To add to the confusion, the programme shows that some riders had only two rides and one had none – so maybe it didn't matter too much at the time, a big, speedway-starved crowd enjoyed some great racing and I'm sure riders and spectators wanted to celebrate the return of the sport they had been deprived of for so long.

So, there we have it. Mystery solved thanks to Kevin and John.

Additional material: Norman Jacobs and Speedway Researcher.

Chapter 52
SQUIB STANDS TALL

YOU may have heard the tale of how the great American speedway showman Lloyd 'Sprouts' Elder got the name Sprouts.

It was because, as a young man, he was small in stature and had ambitions to become a jockey. But he sprouted, and became so tall that they called him . . . well, you know the rest . . . he turned himself into an early star of the cinder tracks known universally as Sprouts.

Now a similar fate befell Cyril Frederick Burton who was born at Crossington, Leicestershire on January 16 1908. He is the rather tall gentleman in riding leathers cuddling that trophy in the picture.

Cyril was so small as a child it led to some contemporary wags nicknaming him 'Squib'. Then he confounded them all by reaching 6ft 1in as an adult, eventually growing clean out of all that hair you see in the picture. Like Sprouts, he went on to become a famous international cinder-shifter. But the name stuck and he was always known as Squib Burton.

Squib began his speedway career at the early Coventry track at Foleshill, transferring to Leicester in the Autumn of 1928 where he rode in the novice class. Obviously talented, it was not long before he had progressed to senior racing, transferring to Rochdale, winning several individual competitions in 1929, including breaking the world record for

Cuddling his cup. A very young Squib – with hair – and one of his early trophies.

This is how he did it. Squib in spectacular full flowing style at High Beech in 1931.

Squib is in the centre of the Hackney line-up at Waterden Road. From the left there is Cliff Parkinson, Morian Hansen, Squib, Dick Case, Mick Murphy, Fred Evans (manager) and Herbet 'Dusty' Haigh. I can't name the rider with his head down next to Squib.

four laps over a quarter of a mile with a time of 89.4 seconds.

Squib was a bit of a nomad, switching back to Leicester In 1930 where he was the side's number one. It was Lea Bridge in 1931 because Leicester folded.

He was part of the England team that faced Australia for all but the first of the historic first official five-match Test series in 1930, going on to tour New Zealand as part of the England side that winter.

Back in Britain he joined Sheffield in 1932 but returned to Lea Bridge, and when they folded he moved on to Walthamstow in 1934 and then Hackney in 1935. A series of injuries led to Squib retiring from speedway, although he went on to race midget cars.

Among his other accomplishments was winning the first race at Donington Park in 1931. The bike he rode is now exhibited in the National Motor Museum. Fifty years later he donated his trophy from that race to the Donington Park Racing Association Club. It was subsequently known as the Squib Burton Challenge Trophy and awarded to the highest scoring British rider at the British Superstock Championship rounds at Donington.

In 1950 Squib resumed his speedway connection when he became the manager at Leicester. He ran a garage at Lutterworth where he was also a magistrate. Squib died in 1990 aged 82.

In the Leicester team of 1950 are Johnny Carpenter, Jock Grierson, Les Beaumont, Ron Wilson, Jack Watts, Jack Winstanley, Joe Bowkis, Vic Pitcher and Squib. Seated: Cyril Page, Reg Morgan, Harwood Pike, Pedlar Palmer.

Chapter 53
WHY ROY'S CAREER NEVER REALLY TOOK OFF

NOW this is a JAP engine . . . when you have speedway stars in your eyes and ambitions to seek fame and fortune in probably the toughest sport in the world, you can't beat a few words of wisdom from someone who has done it all and is the sport's top expert on the JAP.

The young man in the leathers and helmet apparently listening with wrapped attention to the sage instructions he is being given is Roy Uden who, before the war, had been a fairly well known grass track rider and had tried to make the switch to speedway at the old Dagenham Sunday track in 1939, later riding in wartime meetings at Rye House.

The picture dates from about 1947 and was taken at Rye House, which had become a nursery track used by all the big metropolitan clubs to bring on promising youngsters.

Roy, though, was hardly a youngster at the time, being 30 years old. But he did make it into Plymouth's Third Division side the following year, moving on to non league Rayleigh who were then running open meetings.

One of Roy's outstanding characteristics was his luxuriant 'Flying Office Kite' moustache, and his career appeared to be taking off with averages of five and 6.67 over two seasons. But he never quite made it. He broke a leg in a crash against Leicester at the Weir in 1950 and never got going again, but when he recovered he became Rayleigh team manager.

In contrast Wal Phillips tasted life at the top. He was a gatecrasher at the historic first meeting at High Beech in 1928 and became one of the aristocrats of the game.

Wal began his speedway career in 1929 at Stamford Bridge helping them to win the Southern League Championship. He was a member of the England side in the historic first official Test against Australia in 1930 and appeared in the Star Championship Final in 1932, then the equivalent of a World Championship. Stamford Bridge closed that year and the entire team went to Wimbledon. Wal qualified for the first official World Final in 1936, then a broken leg at the Sydney Showground during the 1936/37 England tour of Australia ended his racing career.

He remained as Dons' team manager up to the war and when Harringay reopened in 1947 became team manager and technical chief for the Racers.

Wal took a leading part in the development of the JAP engine and was awarded a gold star for lapping the Brooklands motor racing track at more than 100mph on a JAP. After he shattered the Stamford Bridge track record on his JAP the motor went on to dominate the sport into the 1960s. He also developed a fuel injection system and produced a lay-down speedway machine in 1948.

He was President of the World Speedway Riders Association in 1968.

Chapter 54
AUSSIES WITH THE GLOVES OFF...

CAN you spot the deliberate mistakes being made by these two riders? I'll give you a clue: the 'Elf 'n' Safety' lobby wouldn't allow it to happen today. Too dangerous.

Before I let you in on their indiscretions – supposing of course that you don't beat me to it and smartly twig their misdemeanours for yourselves – you had better know who they are and their speedway credentials.

They are both from Australia – well, you would expect Australians to mangle a few rules, wouldn't you? It's what they do.

So . . . distinguished by the contrast in the way they are going about their business, they are the great Max Grosskreutz, leg-trailing to the manner born, and putting his best foot forward of those graceful cowhorn handlebars, the one and only Frank Dolan.

For years I laboured under the belief that Max had the most magnificent name in speedway – Maximilian Octavius Grosskreutz. Until I was put severely in my place by being told that Max's name was just . . . Max.

Born in Prosperine, Queensland in 1906 he first worked cutting sugar cane until taking to the track and carving out a distinguished international career with Belle Vue's magnificent team of all the talents in the Thirties.

He quit racing to run Norwich just before the war and then returned to Britain to ride for Odsal until a nasty crash, ironically at Belle Vue in 1948, made him decide to retire. One of the very best speedway stars never to appear in a World Final, he died at 88 in 1994.

Frank Dolan, who possessed film star looks, learned his speedway in Sydney with his friends Vic and Ray Duggan and came to Britain in 1938 to ride for Lea Bridge, Southampton and Harringay.

He was Australian Champion in 1946 and came back to Harringay in 1947 where his scoring rate was second only to the phenomenal Vic Duggan's. Allocated to Odsal with a price tag of a meagre £500 in 1949, he decided he didn't want to leave London and never returned to race in Britain.

. . . Oh yes, I almost forgot. If you take a close look at the pictures you will see that neither Max nor Frank is wearing gloves or a face mask. And neither of those sharp pointed clutch levers has a little safety ball at the end.

Chapter 55
GEMS FROM THE FIVEPENNY BOX

ANYONE among you who has, over the years, done me the honour of pausing occasionally at my modest wayside stall to partake of – with or without a pinch of salt – my genuine homespun tales of speedway antiquity, will almost certainly be acquainted with the famous Fivepenny Box.

If you are of a more recent vintage, and don't know about the Fivepenny Box, let me introduce you.

It was originally the discovery of that long time speedway scribbler and predecessor of mine, the late Basil Storey. Now Basil shuffled off his mortal coil many years ago, but regular readers will know that he is still capable of imposing his celestial presence – and wisdom – on the present day speedway scene, when the spirit moves him.

The delights of the Fivepenny Box first presented themselves to Basil during his promenades among the second hand bookshops in London's Charing Cross Road, but the Fivepenny Box can be spotted and enjoyed at any local rummage sale or charity emporium where you will find an old shoe box – or similar – full of dog-eared and well thumbed paperbacks costing, in my day – and Basil's – no'but five copper coins of the realm to acquire.

That was then, of course. As this is now the price has gone up rather somewhat. If you're lucky and come upon a sale day you can pick up any volume that catches your eye for a mere 50p – ten times the old price. Or it could be 'five for £1' – which is twenty times what used to go for 5p . . . but of course you may consider you get more for your money.

However, I digress.

During one of Basil's forays he unearthed a little volume entitled *Meet Them With Us*, a sort of unpretentious pre-war *Who's Who Of Speedway*. The authors called themselves Gar Harrow and Hal Seer.

Meet Them With Us is unique in two ways. First because it details the very human and whimsical nature of the people then involved in speedway racing. You will see, if you observe the modern legendary speedway heroes at your local track, that their characters differ hardly at all from those of the men written bout in the days when Messrs Harrow and Seer earned a crust by slaving over their hot typewriters.

Secondly it is unique because the book's full title is Meet Them With Us – Part One. The original was published in the momentous year of 1939, just in time for the war to put the kibosh on almost everything to do with speedway, which explains why the names of the personalities listed therein reach only those beginning with the letter 'E'.

Unfortunately, after 78 years we are still waiting for a subsequent edition to make an appearance. Tom Morgan, who used to write for *The People* newspaper under the name of *Broadsider* made a valiant attempt to fill the void in 1949 with his *Who's Who Of Speedway*, and my colleague Peter Oakes has also made attempts at redress over the years. But there has nothing really to compare with *Meet Them With Us – Part One*, as I shall now demonstrate.

In their introduction Mr Harrow and Mr Seer say: 'We have written a book which endeavours to parade before you the colourful personalities, riders and officials, who have contributed to . . . speedway racing in this country. It is hoped that it will be found both

*Below left:
The unique, unpretentious and unmistakable cover of the pre-war who's who of speedway,* Meet Them With Us - Part One, *price ninepence – that's 3.75p in today's money.*

Below right: The main men for the 1939 World Championship paraded by Messrs Harrow and Seer, Lionel Van Praag, Jack Milne, Cordy Milne and Wilbur Lamoreaux.

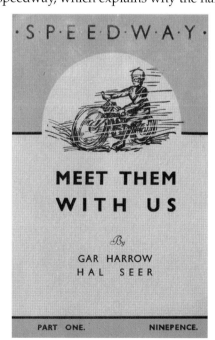

Four of the most successful World's Championship qualifiers line up for the Final at Wembley. From left to right : Lionel Van Praag, Jack Milne, Cordy Milne, and Wilbur Lamoreaux.

Ernie Evans, who enjoyed 'a new lease of life'.

entertaining and useful.'

A modest hope indeed, and one amply fulfilled. It does contain a wealth of information and, at an original cost of the princely sum of nine (old) pence, proved popular enough to be reprinted within a month of publication – a fact that is likely to turn current authors of speedway books a virulent shade of green. Me included.

And of speedway's future they say: 'Twelve years of prolonged endeavour, and argument, with the accent on the latter, have brought us a tolerably stable sport which, despite certain setbacks may, to those imbued with reasonable optimism, be considered to have prospects of expansion in coming years.'

Or: Always look on the bright side of life . . .

But, when you get into the book, who could possibly resist being drawn in to such tantalising headlines as these, for instance?

Bother Over Birthplace – South African Born Australian Who Took New Lease Of Life . . .

That's about Ernie Evans who rode for Wimbledon, Sheffield and New Cross.

Or:

Twelve summonses At 16 – Ran Two Motorbikes before His father Even Knew He Could Ride

That's about former Bristol favourite George Craig

Or:

Hero Worship Made Him A Star Master Versus Pupil : A Secret Marriage

That's about how Malcolm Craven got his start in speedway, was matched against his schoolboy hero veteran Colin Watson . . . and married in secret.

Or:

Speedway's Crash King – Rode In Test With Five Fractured Ribs And Broken Ankle

Big time Ernie in the 1939 Australian line-up. From left: Nobby Clarke, Ron Johnson, Vic Duggan, Lionel Van Praag on the bike, Andy Menzies, Ray Duggan, Arthur Simcock, manager, Ernie, Eric Collins and Aub Lawson.

George Craig in the 1950 Swindon side. From the left: Danny Malone, Ron Clark, Reg Whitcomb, promoter, Alex Gray on the bike, George, Reg Lambourne, Frank Evans, Bob Jones, Hugh Geddes kneeling.

That's about the one and only King Of Crash, Phil Bishop of High Beech, Clapton, Harringay and West Ham.

And:

School friend Of Vic Huxley – Butcher boy turned star

That one tells the story of Eric Collins of Wimbledon.

As Mr Harrow and Mr Seer so astutely point out, 'speedway is essentially a sport of personalities.' In many other sports, they observe, individuals count for little and in many branches of motor sport it is the machine which counts most.

'In speedway it is different,' they say. 'The machine is important, undeniably so. But so is the man who rides it. While team riding is not a negligible consideration, individualism has caused the sport to almost feverishly develop its personalities.' Right from the off *Meet them With Us – Part One* is a book of contrasts. It shows contrast in styles. There is Ernie Evans furiously leg-trailing across the pages, while opposite him is the great Canadian Jimmy Gibb (motto: Never Gibb Up) demonstrating the foot forward technique.

Triumph is represented by a shot of four of the main contenders for the ill-fated 1939 World Final, cancelled by the war. They are all lined up in their quaint plain black leathers, with never a sponsor's logo in sight. Lionel Van Praag, Jack and Cordy Milne and Wilbur Lamoreaux.

They were the stars, the champions. But who, these days remembers the lesser lights? Men, for instance like Roy Dook. Roy was never a star, but he rode with the big stars. I remember him fondly as a member of the Birmingham 'team of trailers' in the first racing season after the war. His career went right back to speedway's beginnings.

Left: *The master. Malcolm the post-war accomplished performer at West Ham in 1947. He never gave up his distinctive narrow turned down handlebars.*

Far left: *The pupil. A very young Malcolm Craven during his pre-war time at Wembley showing off his trophies.*

The King Of Crash living up to his name. Phil Bishop and Roy Dook in a tangle at High Beech.

He started winning races at Lea Bridge a fortnight after getting his first rides in August 1928, chalking up some notable victories over the Frogley brothers.

But let Messrs Harrow and Seer tell the Roy Dook story. 'From Lea Bridge Roy moved to Coventry. Then, when the Crystal Palace club moved to New Cross in 1934 Roy came down from the Midlands with Stan Greatrex to join Ron Johnson & Co.

'Roy never became outstanding and in 1937 moved to Bristol where he assisted the West Country club to a very successful season in which the League Championship was won. That effort earned Bristol promotion to the First Division in 1938, but Roy found the pace too hot in senior circles and after a modest season at Bristol returned to the Second Division. Most of the big stars departed for the 1939 season, but Roy stayed on to command a regular pace in the team.

'Essentially a safe rider who avoided serious accidents, Roy is one of those reliable fellows who got through a considerable amount of work without hitting the headlines.'

And then our two intrepid authors deliver a throwaway line at the end of this mini-

The King Of Crash Phil Bishop, demonstrating his spectacular style when he manages to stay on the bike and out of trouble.

biography – possibly the most fascinating fact about Roy Dook I have ever heard. They reveal: 'He is an inquiry agent away from speedway racing.'

Well, well. What do you know? Roy Dook a private eye. I never knew that before. I certainly can't recall any other speedway gumshoes, can you?

The last name in the book is Norman Evans who first made an appearance on the speedways at Middlesbrough in 1928 and later became associated with New Cross, Harringay and the great Newcastle sides of the immediate post war years.

At Harringay before the war the Parker brothers, Jack and Norman, used to call him 'Pansy' Evans because he was a smart, dapper man who used to dress with impeccable taste, sometimes sporting a French style black beret – ostensibly to disguise his lack of hair.

But he was tough with it and, according to Norman Parker you could hit Pansy Evans with a good punch in the solar plexus and he would never even catch his breath.

'Pansy,' reveal our well-known double act Harrow and Seer, 'is a

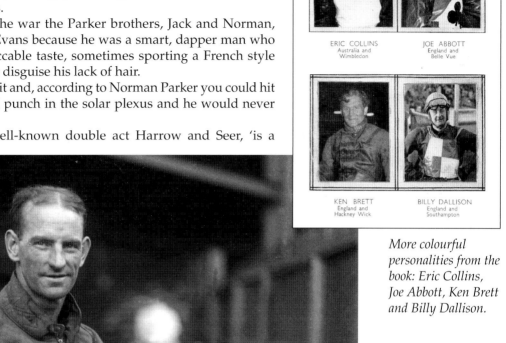

ERIC COLLINS
Australia and
Wimbledon

JOE ABBOTT
England and
Belle Vue

KEN BRETT
England and
Hackney Wick

BILLY DALLISON
England and
Southampton

More colourful personalities from the book: Eric Collins, Joe Abbott, Ken Brett and Billy Dallison.

Norman 'Pansy' Evans . . . can you wonder how he got the name, even though he was 'smart, dapper and dressed with impeccable taste'?

Butcher boy: Eric Collins.

Private eye in the 1938 Bristol line-up with, from left, Morain Hansen, Vic Duggan, Bill Clibbett, Cordy Milne on the bike, Ronnie Greene promoter, Roy, Harry Shepherd and Bill Rogers.

practical joker, a good swimmer and very fond of playing cards – especially on long train journeys. He is married an generally happy.'

Hardly anyone could ask for anything better than that.

But there is another fascinating fact – about the authors. My friend Basil admitted to knowing next to nothing about Mr Harrow, and very little more about Mr Seer, except that he had chosen to have his name spelled backwards, for some unaccountable reason, and it was really Rees.

Anyway, having read about this gem of a discovery at the time, it naturally came as something of a thrill for me when at last a copy of this fascinating and informative book came into my possession recently.

But, as you can guess, it set me back a bit more than five pence.

The practical joker… Norman as captain of the 1948 Newcastle team. His bike is being leaned on by the master practical joker, Johnnie Hoskins. Others are, from the left: Peter Lloyd, Ken LeBreton, Alec Grant, Jackie Hunt, Danny Calder, Charlie Spinks, Eddie 'Crusty' Pye, Wilf Jay and Keith Gurtner.

Chapter 56
HOW FRED CAME TO HAVE AN ANGEL ON HIS ARM

YOU would think, to look at the gentleman in the picture, that far from being a speedway star, he had just gone ten rounds with Mohammed Ali. And lost.

He is that knocked about.

But . . . if you believe in happy endings . . . he has an angel on his arm. I kid you not.

No, the lady is not about to guide our Fred through the Pearly Gates. When the picture first appeared the headline they put on it was: *They Gave Fred A New Face*.

Fred was Fred Tate, a star of the Hackney Wick team. The picture dates from 1936 when Fred was recovering from a serious crash at Wimbledon. So bad were Fred's facial injuries that the skill of a plastic surgeon was necessary to repair the damage. Fred was given practically a new face.

This in itself is remarkable because plastic surgery technique was in its infancy when Fred had his crash. It would be some years before Sir Archibald McIndoe's pioneering work in plastic surgery helped to rehabilitate RAF fighter pilots horrifically burned in their planes during the Battle of Britain who became known as members of The Guinea Pig Club.

When Fred got banged up, his team mates at Hackney included top liners such as Dicky Case, Bill Clibbett, Squib Burton, Dusty Haigh, George Wilks, Stan Dell, Morian Hansen, Mick Murphy, Frank Hodgson, Cliff Parkinson, Reg Stanley, Phil 'Tiger' Hart and Jack Bibby.

He rode in the Wimbledon qualifier of the World Championship and topped the scores with 11, above team mates Dick Case, Morian Hansen, George Newton of New Cross and future World Champion Wembley's Tommy Price.

Fred was down to ride in the Harringay and West Ham Championship rounds on his way to Wembley and that historic first World Final in 1936, but he did not ride at either meeting – assuredly because he'd had his accident.

The crash finished his riding career, but not his association with the sport. In 1937 he became speedway manager at Nottingham which was a subsidiary of the Hackney Wick company.

So how did Fred come to be the lucky man after all and end up with an angel on his arm? The picture shows him braving the latter day paparazzi and leaving home for a motoring trip with his fiancé Miss Angel Wilson who later became Mrs Tate.

Married to an Angel. How's that for a happy ending?

Chapter 57
HOT SHOT DENNIS!

WHO SACRIFICED HIS CALIFORNIA COMFORT ZONE
FOR THE HELL OF HULL . . . AND BACK

American invaders. The US Test side of sparkling talent at Ipswich in 1982. Standing from the left are Shawn Moran, Dennis, John Scott, manager, Scott Autrey and Ron Preston. Kneeling, John Cook, Bruce Penhall, Bobby Schwartz and Kelly Moran. Their togetherness engendered a notably extraordinary team spirit.

SPEEDWAY racing in Europe, and especially in England, is deep routed in society. Top stars in British speedway can make a handsome living and gain great respect in public life as well as within the sport itself.

If we assume that all this is true – or at least it was when the observation was written originally all of thirteen years ago – it must be asked: why are there now, as then, so many foreign riders contracted to ride in Britain?

The era we are talking about here is just before the turn of the present century and speedway then was overrun – perhaps a better word would be blessed – with Americans. True, we have recently witnessed an outstanding American who won his fourth World Championship. Greg Hancock at the ripe and mature age of 46.

He has by far exceeded the achievements of all the other Americans who went before him. And the reason now, as then, is: Talent with a capital T.

That last comment is an example of homespun philosophy which came from Brad Oxley, whose father Harry – now long retired – revitalised in the 1960s the Southern Californian speedway scene with the help of 1937 World Champion Jack Milne and a couple of multi-title holders from New Zealand, Barry Briggs and Ivan Mauger.

That particular enterprise earned Czar status for Harry. His tough and uncom-

promising family business sense elevated his tiny speedway citadel at Costa Mesa, on the south side of Los Angeles, to international renown. It produced a tsunami of hugely gifted young men who together put an unprecedented gloss on the sport worldwide.

That all-star line-up of talent that came out of West Coast USA included DeWayne Keeter, Steve Gresham, Scott Autrey, Steve and Mike Bast, Bobby 'Boogaloo' Schwartz, Kelly and Shawn Moran, Shawn 'Mad Dog' McConnell, Steve Lucero, Sudden Sam Ermolenko, Rick Miller, Ronnie Correy, Ron Preston, John 'Cowboy' Cook, Mike 'The Bud Man' Faria, Billy Hamill. And of course, Mr Glamour himself, the Main Man until Hancock, Bruce Penhall.

Brad Oxley's observations are valid because he too paid his speedway dues in England. Big Bad Brad told one interviewer that the time he spent at Wimbledon was 'two years of living in a slum. It really taught me to appreciate living in the States'. Clearly he is as uncompromisingly outspoken as his father and now has succeeded Harry to carry on the business.

Brad was convinced all that sparkling speedway talent was nurtured by 'guys handlebar knocking' most nights on the tiny Stateside circuits. If you have ever seen speedway SoCal style you would have to agree with him. Plus the fact that 'Second and Third Division riders got to race on the same programme as the more established star riders, exposing them to real racing and inspiring them to do more each race'.

A graduate of that Hot Shot Academy was Dennis Sigalos who, when ancient veterans like me gather to argue over who were the best riders never to win an individual World Championship, has to be near the top of that privileged list.

Along with such legendary names as: Vic Huxley, Vic Duggan and Graham Warren of Australia, Wilbur Lamoreaux and Cordy Milne of America, Jack Parker, Kenny Carter and Brian Crutcher of England, Sverre Harrfeldt of Norway, Zenon Plech of Poland, Tommy Knudsen of Denmark . . . We could all go on, so fill in with your own favourite.

Except that Dennis Sigalos, who spent all too little time in European speedway – five full seasons and part of two others – was more talented than most. After all, at the last count he is a five times World Champion . . . though at powerboating. Of which more later.

The great tragedy is that his racing career was ended prematurely in the Long Beach World Championship qualifier in June 1984, in a bizarre crash which virtually destroyed an ankle.

So what was the original attraction of speedway? Dennis started racing pedal cycles, waxing the garage floor and sliding them.

Cover boy: Dennis on the front of the American Speedway Magazine *taking precedence – for once – over 'the main man', Bruce Penhall as he appeared in the television highway patrol saga CHiPS.*

Los Angeles World Final 1982. It is Heat 12, Penhall leads with Dennis on the outside just over Bruce's shoulder. 'He came out of the turn first and beat me,' Dennis remembered. Following them is England's Dave Jessup whose engine failed and allowed Poland's Edward Jancarz to take third place.

Culture shock. For the Americans England was a radical change from their sunshine and beach lifestyle and they wisely covered up. From the left they are: Bobby Schwartz, Kelly Moran, John Cook, with his back to the camera, Bruce Penhall, John Scott, the back of Shawn Moran, Dennis and Scott Autrey.

Dennis said: 'The attraction was the speed and getting sideways. It started on bicycles at the age of ten or eleven. Then, by the age of 12, Bruce and I started riding junior speedway bikes that had McCullough chainsaw engines. When I was thirteen I started riding a 500cc two-valve JAWA at an outlaw track until I was sixteen when I could ride at Costa Mesa. Until then we rode the junior bikes at Costa Mesa at half time along with Shawn and Kelly Moran who rode their mini-bikes.

'We also practised at Saddleback. Then Bruce's father built a track on some vacant land at my father's business, Orange County Food Services at Anaheim. The track started out basic, but we ended up with a clay base and a decomposed granite surface with crashwalls. George Wenn made us some starting gates, we had an electric generator out there and we converted an old catering truck with a water tank to water the track. We practised there all the time.'

According to what I had read about Dennis I got the impression that he didn't really need to rely on speedway for a living because the family was, shall we say, quite comfortably off.

He said: 'Dad has a food distribution business. He has worked hard. He has catering trucks and vending machines. It's been a family business since 1942. Dad bought us bikes, but I have always worked. Long days, early mornings, late nights.'

The late Ipswich promoter John Berry said that when he went to America to interview Dennis about signing for the Witches the young man turned up in a Ferrari Boxter. 'That was my Dad's car' said Dennis. 'My car was a 1984 Mercedes that I brought back from France, but I normally drove my company car, a Chevvy Malibu. My wife has the good car.'

So, after junior racing Dennis had started to attract the attention of overseas promotions. What was the atmosphere like on the US speedway scene at that time?

Dennis said: 'Bruce and I started racing full time in 1973. I started in Division Three and the following week moved up to Division Two. After another couple of weeks I was riding Division One. At that time speedway was big. Rick Woods, Sonny Nutter, Wild Bill Cody, Dennis 'Berserko' Becker – those guys were our idols. We went to the races every Friday night. Once we started racing we followed the circuit: Ventura, San Bernardino, Irwindale, Bakersfield, Costa Mesa. So you could race five or six nights a week if you wanted to.'

The top star at the time was seven times USA National Champion Mike Bast, who was earning quite well then. So how easy was it for Dennis to leave and travel to take his chances in Europe?

Sometimes the English weather can be unkind to speedway riders but there were nights when Dennis, and his two helpers, just had to get on with it.

*Contemplation.
Sometimes you could
be left wondering
exactly why you
did it.*

*But there was always
the lighter side. John
Cook and Dennis
were always a comic
double act to keep
their team mates'
morale up high.*

'When I first started it was a couple of hundred dollars for winning a main event,' said Dennis. 'Then, for a top rider, it got up to maybe $600 or $1,000 a night. For a kid leaving home, going off in a van every evening with a couple of motorcycles, it was good money. I didn't go to England for the money, I went for the experience. I was in a position to go ahead and check it out.'

So why, when he did get to England, was he associated with Hull? He said: 'Someone, I don't recall who, came along with Ole Olsen and met me. I had just returned from Australia and someone there had recommended me. I don't know why I picked Hull. Ian Thomas and Brian Larner ran the place. I lived in Easington, on the North Sea. It was a hell of a journey driving everywhere from Hull, especially to Poole and Exeter.'

Then he left Hull for Ipswich. Did John Berry offer him a better deal?

'Yes, but I don't remember all the details,' said Dennis. 'Ipswich was geographically better because it mean more racing and less travel time. I moved to Bucklesham, near Ipswich. I got along great with John. I think I had only one argument. He always treated me fairly. I got to be team captain which was great. He was able to promote me, it enabled my whole career to take off.'

Fan fodder. And Dennis never failed to oblige with a smile.

Once in Europe there appeared to be some criticism back home that he didn't return to race there as often as some of the others – Bruce, Bobby, John Cook etc. The US speedway establishment – headed by Czar Oxley – maybe justifiably considered that the talent they had nurtured and exported to became real international stars, were valuable assets and should have returned regularly to race before the local fans. In fact there was a system of compulsory returns.

'Not to start with,' said Dennis. 'It was a big expense to fly back and forth. I returned the last few years when the American Motorcycle Association (AMA) paid for it. I loved to get home. In the early years we had to pay our own air fares.'

Dennis was not afraid to be outspoken. For instance it was reported that in one interview he said he was just as good as Penhall but Bruce had had all the luck. He also said that American fans went to the races to enjoy themselves. British fans went to the races to get drunk.

'No. I never said that. I would probably say the opposite,' said Dennis. 'British fans take their racing much more seriously. We all got into rows with British fans who supported their rider such as Ole Olsen. Kenny Carter's fans were the worst. As far as Bruce and I were concerned, we are both highly competitive. Either of us could beat the other on any given day.'

To me, Dennis seemed very self possessed. I suspected speedway technique came rather naturally to him. But did he have any idols, was there anyone who influenced him, who he wanted to be like?

'Yes. Rick Woods was my idol when I first started out. I even copied the stripes on his leathers,' said Dennis. 'Then, after that I followed Ivan Mauger. Another reason for going to Hull was because Ivan was there. There was no one better. Getting to ride with him was a real experience. He would prefer the inside start position and I ended up liking the outside.

'Mike Bast influenced my riding. We had kind of similar riding styles. Then obviously Bruce and Bobby went over to England first, so I learned a lot from them.'

Dennis Sigalos, to me, seemed not only a very stylish rider but also a very safe one. He appeared to be lucky to escape serious injury – except for the career ending incident at Long Beach – though I did see someone plough into the back of him at Hackney one night which catapulted him into the wire fence (no air fences then) yet he walked away from that totally unscathed. Did the dangers of the sport ever occur to him and, if so, did it bother him?

A better deal and the travelling was easier. Dennis considered it 'great' to be made captain of Ipswich. This is the 1983 team, from the left: Andy Hibbs, Billy Sanders, Jeremy Doncaster, Preben Erikssen, Nigel Flatman, Andy Hines, Dennis on bike.

Leading from the front, as a captain should. Dennis shows partner Mike Lanham the way as they get ahead of Cradley Heath's Bent Rassmussen, outside, and Andy Graham.

'No it didn't bother me at the time,' Dennis said. 'Obviously you want to be safe but you have to ride on the edge if you want to progress. I guess riding came naturally to me because I started to so young. My style might have been different because I am taller than most speedway riders. I certainly did not want to put my neck on the line too much. You have to be able to come back and do it tomorrow.

'After Long Beach it didn't feel the same. I'd had enough of travelling, being away from home, getting older. I started to think about work and a regular job.

'I got ploughed into at Ipswich after that. John Berry brought me back for the Knockout Cup. In my first race back after breaking my ankle I was in third place and some young Swedish guy tried to go round me and I ended up getting my foot stuck in his chain. I got seven stitches in that.

'I had a few crashes that hurt, but was lucky not to break any bones. I got tangled up with Bobby at Cradley Heath and caught my ankle bone in the clutch nut, where you tighten the clutch. It clipped my bone. Then two weeks later I had to race for the World Championship and had to cut off the cast for that. Earlier I got a dislocated shoulder, but a lot of riders get that when they go off the high side. I do consider myself lucky overall.'

Dennis was always a very fair rider too, yet there was an incident with Hans Nielsen of Denmark at London White City in a World Championship qualifier. Dennis lifted, got in Hans's way and he ended up in the fence. Words were obviously exchanged and I wondered what really happened there.

'I remember that to this day,' said Dennis. 'Because he was a baby at that time. I was leading and found traction and got in a wheelie. When I came down I bobbled and Hans tried to go round me. He may have run into me or just got close and laid it down, then went into the fence and lay there like it was a big problem.

'I told him to get up, it was not my fault. That's all I said to him. I got excluded and thought it was unfair. Generally I am not a too outspoken kind of guy. I like to be fair. I was there to race, not to run people off the road.'

And then there was that rumpus in the 1982 White City qualifier when Penhall 'threw' the race so that Dennis and Kelly Moran could progress towards the World Final in Los Angeles.

'Bruce would never throw a race,' said Dennis. 'Absolutely not. It was a tough day and I think one of us was going to go out and it could have been two. Bruce wanted to help everyone out and maybe didn't race as hard as he could have, which helped Kelly, maybe Bobby and myself. I don't remember exactly now. I think it was Shawn who didn't make it through.'

In an advert in one magazine I once counted that Dennis had 27 sponsors and a back-up team of 16, plus three Debbies, his girlfriend, sister and stepmother. Did he find it easy to attract sponsors, and what kind of assistance did they give – was it cash or kind?

'Mostly product,' said Dennis. 'One of my biggest was Pepsi and they did give me some money. I got that through my Dad's business since we were a big user of Pepsi products

The reckoning. Bruce 'Main Man' Penhall tops the World Championship rostrum for the second time at Los Angeles and Dennis finished third – 'it could have been anyone's night' – and England's Les Collins was second.

and I was marketable to them. Most of the others were product. Bell gave me helmets, Oakley gave me goggles, a little cash here and there.

'Basically I was living on profits from racing, just like most of the guys. There were exceptions. Bruce did real well, but he was more marketable than a lot of people.

'I am down to two Debbies now. My Dad is no longer married to his Debbie.'

For many Americans European speedway and its attendant lifestyle was a bit of a culture shock. I called in at Bobby Schwartz's house in England early one morning and found Dennis fast asleep in a chair – not in a bed – and some girl propped up asleep in another chair in the corner. Was that, I wondered, pretty much what life was like for a travelling speedway star?

'Yes. Most of the time we were travelling, staying in hotels, sleeping on ferries,' said Dennis. 'We spent a lot of time in each other's houses. The houses were small, there was a limited number of beds, so sometimes you got to sleep on the floor. I don't remember that incident. It must have been innocent if we were in different ends of the room.'

There was supposed to be an extraordinary team spirit among the Americans in Britain at that time.

'There was tremendous morale among all the Americans over here,' said Dennis. 'At first Scott Autrey was still there, then there was Bobby, Bruce, Steve Gresham, Ronnie

The All-American speedway star. Dennis checks out the action at a World Championship qualifier at White City London, Kenny 'I hate Americans' Carter is standing right next to him.

Preston, Kelly, Shawn. We formed the US team. I still have one of the jackets with the patches.

'That's when we started the US v England series. Maybe the first or second year I was there. We used to go to each other's houses, we used to drive fast cars, drive on the beach, play a little golf, we had a great time together.

'When I lived at Ipswich, Felixstowe was just down the road. We used to go water skiing. Cookie (John Cook) and I made friends with Americans at the local air force base. Billy Sanders was in Ipswich, we hung out with him a lot.

'Around that time I raced a Formula Ford and won my first race at Snetterton. The guy who built my speedway engines did a lot of work on Formula Ford. I told him that if he was ever short of a driver I would like to give it a try. Something happened to one of the drivers, he broke both his ankles, so they asked me if I would like to check it out.

'I practised and raced the next day. I qualified third but didn't make a good start and got up to second. Then there was a big crash and it got red-flagged. In the restart I got a good start and won from wire to wire. I later did another race at Brands Hatch, Formula Ford Festival, about 300 entries. I got eleventh and missed the final by one place.'

The World Team Cup and World Pairs seemed to be a breeze for Dennis – especially when he blew away all the opposition with Bobby in the World Pairs at Liverpool in Australia. That was the year America did the Grand Slam and won all the world titles – yet I was surprised that Dennis appeared in only two individual World Finals. His declared ambition had been to win the individual title. Was it a disappointment for it not to happen?

He said: 'The World Pairs final in Australia was a wonderful trip. The whole thing came together. We based ourselves at Nigel Boocock's house. It was a great night. We had shipped over the right Carlisle tyres. We made every start. Billy Sanders almost got us, but the referee flagged the race and restarted it. We had ridden the track before and we deserved to win that night.

'Sure I was disappointed over the World Finals, but at the same time, looking back, I accomplished a lot.'

What about those two World Finals . . . the Los Angeles one in 1982 must have been very special to all the American riders. Dennis finished third. How did he remember the meeting and how did he feel about third place? He must have wanted to win it badly, but Bruce did, and for the second time.

The start of a bit of trouble. Dennis lifts in the 1983 World Championship Intercontinental Final at White City London with Denmark's Hans Nielsen making an outside pass.

Then the action gets a little out of hand. Dennis seems to be back under control, but there appears to be contact and Nielsen is on the way down.

Then the action gets a little out of hand. Dennis seems to be back under control, but there appears to be contact and Nielsen is on the way down.

'Absolutely. I wanted to win it bad,' said Dennis. 'It could have been anyone's night. Bruce was on, making the starts. I remember when I lined up, he was my buddy, but when push comes to shove, he came out of the turn first and he beat me. Les Collins and Kenny Carter beat me also.

'I was proud to get on the rostrum in front of my own home crowd. I had a lot of support. I had busloads of fans. Even my grandparents were there. It was really special.'

Then, of course, there was Norden in Germany in 1983. Everyone seemed to be demoralised by Egon Muller that day.

Dennis said: 'Man, I was demoralised from the first race. I might not have been the favourite to win but I was right up there. I picked the wrong gear in the first race and just got smoked by everyone. After that I just couldn't get back in the rhythm. It was a big, long track, real heavy and thick. I just couldn't get it together.

'Again I had a lot of support. I had my family fly over, Bruce was doing the commentating. Egon was on that day. He was used to those big long tracks. He made it look easy. He deserved to win.

Dennis finished eighth, but he really joined speedway's elite by winning the Czech Golden Helmet in 1983. That must have been very satisfying – but is the helmet solid gold?

'I'm looking at it right now in my trophy case. It is not solid gold,' said Dennis, 'it's gold plated. They are not actually rubies on it, but they look like rubies. Yes, it's unreal. I think I'm the only American to have one.'

The accident at Long Beach came the following year which pretty well seemed to destroy an ankle and with it his career. What, I wondered, did he recall of that?

He said: 'That is exactly what happened. I wasn't having the best of nights. We were using the smaller tyres that were cut down, the knobs weren't as tall and there was less traction. It was my third race. I think I had got a win and a second, or maybe two seconds, so I needed a win. I was second behind Sam Ermolenko, he parked it and I was going to T-bone him.

'Instead I threw it sideways and it just looped all the way round and spat me off the back. I landed on my ankle. I have a picture of me landing. I was out of action for six or eight months. I had broken or dislocated the back part of the heel. They were afraid the bone was going to die.

'Another doctor decided to pin it and put me in a cast, then attached a new machine that worked with magnetic impulses. It was like two pingpong paddles that were velcroed to my ankle. It had a plastic knob that stuck out at the side and I clipped this paddle on there and strapped it round my foot and slept with it at night. It was supposed to stimulate the blood. I did that for months and it healed fine.

'Now it's OK, but in the morning it's sore and it cracks, but I have movement in my ankle.'

But, before the crash, he had been thinking of quitting. Was he maybe bored with

The confrontation. An irate Neilsen exchanges words with Dennis, who remembered: 'He lay there like it was a big problem. I told him to get up, it wasn't my fault. I got excluded and thought it was unfair'.

speedway. He did ride eight matches for Ipswich in 1985 but the scores were down – was it just not possible to continue?

'I came back in '85 for the Knockout Cup,' said Dennis. 'I was out of shape and I hadn't been on a bike for a long time. The first night back at Ipswich I got taken off. I had to ride a day later. It was not fun anymore. I was getting tired of travelling. Not only back and forth to America, but to Europe too. I did not ride for European teams, but rode in individual events most weekends. Germany, Hungary, Italy, Poland.'

What, I wondered, would Dennis consider the high point of his career – the thing he will always remember?

'Obviously the World Pairs championship and the Golden Helmet. Being on the podium at the Coliseum with my Buddy Bruce and Les Collins.'

And the lowest point?

'Breaking my ankle was the worst.' Dennis said. 'Being at Hull at the end of the season knowing that everyone at home was at the beach. The incident with Hans Nielsen.

'Regrets? None whatsoever. The brakes went on when I broke my ankle. I had a car

More trouble at San Bernardino. For someone who claims to be 'a not too outspoken guy', there appears to be a difference of opinion here between Dennis, in his Hull race jacket, and San Bernardino referee Irwin Moon. Both parties seem to be making a forceful point.

Not the best of nights at Long Beach. Dennis, in attempting to avoid running into Sam Ermolenko, the bike 'spat me off the back' and the landing virtually destroyed an ankle. It also virtually destroyed his speedway career.

racing deal lined up in Scotland. Maybe that could have turned into another career. Overall I have no regrets.'

Yet he went on to win World Powerboat Championships with Penhall. How did that come about?

'A friend took us to a powerboat race at Long Beach,' Dennis said. 'Friends of ours had these big, fat offshore boats. That got our interest. A few months later my Dad bought a 38ft pleasure boat. It went about 80 mph, so he and I did one race up at Lake Mead and that was fun. Then Bruce was at a World Championship at Corpus Christie. He called me and said he was having fun and we had to decide how we could do this.

'When he got back we talked some more and decided to get into it. We built a four seater and Ocean Spray came along, again through my Dad's business, and we painted their name on it, got some money from them. Roger Stull, the owner of Bruce's Dad's old company, came up with some money too. We went out in the first race and beat the World Champion at Dana Point. We thought: what a lot of fun. Next we went to Sarasota, then did the circuit. We were hooked.

'We raced for three years, won three World Championships with that boat. This was in nice locations like Galveston, Texas, Key West, Miami, Fort Lauderdale, West Palm Beach. Quite a step up from Hull.

'After the first year we started being marketable and a couple of years later we were approached by Fountain Power Boats who ended up building us another boat which we took to another two World Championships. That one did 90 mph at that time, and Ocean Spray stayed with us the whole time.

Career ending, but not world ending. Dennis jokes on the Fullerton golf course, Los Angeles, during his rehabilitation. And the ankle injury didn't get in the way of his five Powerboat World Championships . . . with – wouldn't you know it – Bruce Penhall.

'Then clothing sponsors came on board with team uniforms, hats, T-shirt sales. It all helped to pay the bills. We did everything in organising it and did road trips using a big freightliner to tow the boat. It was half workshop, half motor home. We were lucky to be able to take time from our day jobs, me from the food service company and Bruce from his sunglasses business.'

Dennis is now back with the family firm, Orange Country Food Service industrial catering. He said: 'Yes, you put your quarter in. We have soda machines, candy bar machines. I have climbed the corporate ladder, from scrubbing baking pans, emptying vending machines, being a mechanic, supervisor. I am now manager in the catering side.'

Dennis once forecast a big suture for speedway in America. Instead it has not really happened.

'I don't really take much interest in speedway now,' Dennis said. 'I go down to Costa Mesa maybe a couple of times a year. I like to follow how Greg Hancock is doing in the Grands Prix though. We thought speedway would really take off here. It hasn't happened and I really don't know why. I enjoyed my time in the sport and think I was there at a great time for American speedway. The guys I rode with are still my close friends today.'

EPILOGUE

DAVE LANNING 1938 – 2016
THE VOICE OF SPEEDWAY

MY speedway world became immeasurably bleaker and a giant sized gap appeared when Dave Lanning left it.

Big Dave left a giant sized gap because he was a giant – in technique, in journalistic and broadcasting ability, but most of all personality.

You wouldn't have known it if you had chanced to wander into the spotlight of that huge personality that he was in reality a very shy man.

In the end we were both speedway dinosaurs, in love not only with the sport but what we considered its Good Old Days. We lived at opposite ends of the country and were frequently on the telephone to each other to discuss the latest fortunes and disasters that befell speedway as it often lurched – staggered even – into the modern era.

We went back a long way and at one time were Fleet Street colleagues on TV Times Magazine. Our paths also crossed frequently in those days on the road when our newspapers required us to cover important international meetings, and Dave had a never-ending fund of tales, as tall as he was, about his adventures in the far-flung speedway outposts.

His talent for quirky items in his unique gossip column for *Speedway Star* were examples of supreme entertainment. Sometimes, of course, he didn't let the facts get in the way of a good story . . . as he saw it. If it had an angle, Dave could present it in that knock-down-drag-out style that pulled in the punters.

For whatever heaven-sent talent Dave had, he knew how to pull in the punters. And many a speedway track ought to be grateful for how his teams, his gimmicks and his supreme public relations skills, got the paying customers through the turnstiles. He also pulled in the Press. When he was at Reading he always made it his business to know which reporters were in at home meetings, and he never failed to announce their names and their journals before the opening race. Such gestures made them feel they were important – and valued.

Reporter Dave. With five times World Champion Ove Fundin on the steps behind the Wembley pits during a World Final.

From top:
*Gallant Dave.
Singing star Anita Harris gets a helping hand at a British Final with champion Barry Briggs holding the trophy in the background.*

*Mikeman Dave.
Enticing words of wisdom from the original Old Windbag himself, Johnnie Hoskins.*

*Showman Dave.
He was never too dignified to join in the end of season fun when there was the traditional flour fight with his riders.*

Above left: Host Dave. He knew how to attract the biggest stars to speedway – Wolves and England legendary football captain Billy Wright makes a presentation to Ken McKinlay when Dave was in charge at West Ham.

Above right: Working man Dave who liked to be right in amongst it. Here he is, a face in the crowd, reporting on an international event in the company of Sweden's Bernt Persson, England's Ray Wilson and Dave Jessup.

Dave and I would give each other advice. When I was writing my biology of Ove Fundin, because I knew Dave had written a ghost column for the five times World Champion in various magazines, I sought his counsel. He told me that Ove trusted him completely and never instructed him on what to write. Dave said: 'I always wrote what I thought Ove would say – and I never had a complaint.' His counsel was gratefully followed.

It was enormously gratifying when he agreed to write a regular column for me during the years I edited *Vintage Speedway Magazine*. His copy was always brilliantly told, on time, immaculately presented and perfectly typed, because, as far as I know, Dave would never deign to acquaint himself with the computer. And when the magazine staged its speedway evenings at the National Motor Museum at Beulieu, Dave was there, his sparkling personality always put a gloss on the evening for everyone.

I was greatly honoured when he asked me to edit the manuscript of his novel *Cinderfellas: When Speedway Was Rock 'n' Roll* and he confided in me his hopes that it would eventually be made into a film.

His skill as a television commentator is not only universally known, but of course his voice lives on over the airwaves on You Tube, the rest of the world wide web and no end of DVD productions. He and I shared the commentary at the 1987 two-day World Final in Amsterdam. We were stuck up high among the steel girders of the Olympic Stadium. On the occasions when I got the microphone it would not be long before I would feel a not so gentle nudge in the ribs. It was Dave telling me he wanted the mic back. He was a demon for the microphone and I think that was when he was truly happy.

He would frequently demand that I make the journey to his home in Poole to 'imbibe something cool in a glass'. I never made it, but in tribute to the lovely man that he was I raise my glass to him now. It was a privilege to have known him and I will truly miss him. The words are well known, but Dave Lanning 'shall not pass this way again'.

You cannot better an original.

JOHN CHAPLIN